Palgrave Socio-Legal Studies

Series Editor
Dave Cowan, School of Law, University of Cardiff, Cardiff, UK

Editorial Board
Dame Hazel Genn, University College London, London, UK
Fiona Haines, School of Social & Political Sciences, University of Melbourne, Melbourne, VIC, Australia
Herbert Kritzer, University of Minnesota, Minneapolis, MN, USA
Linda Mulcahy, Centre for Socio-Legal Studies, University of Oxford, Oxford, UK
Rosemary Hunter, Kent Law School, University of Kent, Canterbury, UK
Carl Stychin, Institute of Advanced Legal Studies, University of London, London, UK
Mariana Valverde, Centre for Criminology & Socio-Legal Studies, University of Toronto, Toronto, ON, Canada
Sally Wheeler, College of Law, Australian National University, Canberra, ACT, Australia
Senthorun Raj, Manchester Metropolitan University, Manchester, Lancashire, UK

The Palgrave Socio-Legal Studies series is a developing series of monographs and textbooks featuring cutting edge work which, in the best tradition of socio-legal studies, reach out to a wide international audience.

Linda Mulcahy · Anna Tsalapatanis

Digital Justice

Engineering Disadvantage?

Linda Mulcahy
Centre for Socio-Legal Studies
University of Oxford
Oxford, UK

Anna Tsalapatanis
Social Research Institute
University College London
London, UK

ISSN 2947-9274   ISSN 2947-9282   (electronic)
Palgrave Socio-Legal Studies
ISBN 978-3-031-65264-6   ISBN 978-3-031-65265-3   (eBook)
https://doi.org/10.1007/978-3-031-65265-3

© The Editor(s) (if applicable) and The Author(s), under exclusive license to Springer Nature Switzerland AG 2024

This work is subject to copyright. All rights are solely and exclusively licensed by the Publisher, whether the whole or part of the material is concerned, specifically the rights of translation, reprinting, reuse of illustrations, recitation, broadcasting, reproduction on microfilms or in any other physical way, and transmission or information storage and retrieval, electronic adaptation, computer software, or by similar or dissimilar methodology now known or hereafter developed. The use of general descriptive names, registered names, trademarks, service marks, etc. in this publication does not imply, even in the absence of a specific statement, that such names are exempt from the relevant protective laws and regulations and therefore free for general use.
The publisher, the authors and the editors are safe to assume that the advice and information in this book are believed to be true and accurate at the date of publication. Neither the publisher nor the authors or the editors give a warranty, expressed or implied, with respect to the material contained herein or for any errors or omissions that may have been made. The publisher remains neutral with regard to jurisdictional claims in published maps and institutional affiliations.

Cover illustration: © John Rawsterne/patternhead.com

This Palgrave Macmillan imprint is published by the registered company Springer Nature Switzerland AG
The registered company address is: Gewerbestrasse 11, 6330 Cham, Switzerland

If disposing of this product, please recycle the paper.

This book is dedicated to all those who go above and beyond what can be expected of them in supporting members of the public in accessing the justice system and pursuing their case.

Acknowledgements

This work was in part supported by the Economic and Social Research Council [Grant Number ES/V01580X/1]

About This Book

This book explores the many changes to justice systems made possible by technology and considers the extent to which these amount to the radical transformations in improving access to justice that they are often claimed to be. Focusing on the English and Welsh legal system as a central case study, the issues raised are of widespread applicability to other legal systems undergoing digitalisation. This book is organised into five chapters which examine the changes that are taking place, what is meant by digital transformation, what the public gain by it and what they lose. The book concludes by suggesting what radical transformation could look like if the lay user were placed at the centre of the design process.

Contents

1	**Introduction—An Awfully Big Experiment**	1
	Introduction	1
	What Are the Problems Technology Is Meant to Solve? A Brief History of Reform in England and Wales	4
	A Neo-Liberal Dream? Difficult Journeys Into Uncharted Waters	11
	Organisation of this Book	14
	Bibliography	18
2	**What Do We Mean by Technological Innovation in the Justice System?**	21
	Introduction	21
	Towards a Typology of Technological Developments in the Civil Justice System	22
	As If Technology	23
	Enhanced Communication and Engagement	25
	Replacing People	27
	Conclusion	31
	Bibliography	34
3	**What Is Gained When Justice Moves Online?**	37
	Introduction	37
	Journeys into the Legal System	39
	Experiences of Trials and Hearings	41
	Rendering Justice More Open	45
	Conclusion	47
	Bibliography	48
4	**What Is Lost When Justice Moves Online?**	53
	Introduction	53
	The Role of Buildings in the Civic Landscape	56

	Journeys to the Court	59
	Inside The Hearing Room: The Shifting Dynamics of Hearings	61
	The Threat to Open Justice	66
	Digital Disadvantage	67
	Conclusion	69
	Bibliography	71
5	**Conclusion: Towards Inclusive Design**	77
	Introduction	77
	Digital Government and Digital Business	78
	Engaging the Public	82
	Conclusion: How Might a User-Centred Transformation Project Look Different?	85
	Bibliography	89
Index		93

About the Authors

Linda Mulcahy is Statutory Professor of Socio-Legal Studies at Oxford University and Director of the Centre for Socio-Legal Studies. Trained as a lawyer and sociologist her work focuses on empirical accounts of the many ways in which the laity experience the legal system. In a career spanning 35 years, she has interviewed hundreds of litigants, defendants, policymakers, lawyers, judges and mediators.

Dr. Anna Tsalapatanis is a Lecturer in Sociology and Social Policy at the Social Research Institute at University College London. She received her PhD in Sociology from the Australian National University and has a Masters' Degree from the University of Athens. Anna has a range of published work on topics such as access to justice, digital disadvantage, migration, and bureaucracy, with a particular focus on qualitative methods.

Abbreviations

AI	Artificial Intelligence
ADR	Alternative Dispute Resolution
CRT	Civil Resolution Tribunal (Canada)
CVP	Cloud Video Platform (a video hearing platform used in the UK during the pandemic)
HMCTS	His Majesty's Court and Tribunal Service
MoJ	Ministry of Justice (UK)
NAO	National Audit Office
ODR	Online Dispute Resolution
PHSO	Parliamentary and Health Service Ombudsman
TPT	Traffic Penalty Tribunal (UK)
VH Service	Video Hearings Service (HMCTS bespoke video hearing platform)

CHAPTER 1

Introduction—An Awfully Big Experiment

Abstract Recent years have seen an increasing interest in the digitalisation of legal systems across the world. Using the UK as a case study, this chapter charts the many reasons why change was considered necessary and the form it has taken. It examines the problems recent transformations were intended to address as well as the particular values which underpin them. Outlining key themes which are pursued across the book such as the transformation of civic sphere, trust in government, and access to justice for all, the chapter makes the case for a renewed focus on lay participants in the legal system.

Keywords Digitalisation · Online justice · Court reform · Technology · Access to justice

INTRODUCTION

This book explores some of the ways in which technology is changing how justice is delivered, and what is delivered. In the course of examining the rapid changes to justice systems now being implemented across the world, we draw attention to a host of issues about the evolving nature of the concepts of access to justice, due process, participation, procedural justice and open justice when interactions with the legal system are increasingly mediated by machines. Exploration of these evolving concepts compels us to engage in debates on broader issues of interest to social scientists such as trust in the institutions of government, debates about the democratic deficit, digital disadvantage, privatisation of public and civic space and the impact of neo-liberal discourse on the delivery of a vital public service. More specifically we ask, how do the dynamics of pre-trial negotiations, or the ceremony and ritual associated with hearings alter when the people involved do not gather together in a special building? What happens to public and civic space when courthouses and other symbolic buildings disappear from the civic landscape? Who do we leave behind when digital technologies take centre stage in the provision of a public service? What impact is the constantly connected society having on the temporality of law? Who, or what, will be making legal decisions and giving legal advice in the post-human age? How can technology be used to improve people's experience of, and confidence in, the legal system? How can we mitigate against the dangers of the digitally disadvantaged being further marginalised? To what extent is technology being used to replace traditional ways of doing things or to enhance communication where previously there was silence or absence? Is it possible for software programmes to improve the quality of decision-making and advice by enhancing human capability?

The speed at which these changes are occurring can make meaningful reflection challenging as we are compelled to think about the day to day and long-term significance of rapid transitions from the industrial to the information age. Mobile technology, increasing bandwidth, nanotechnology, smartphones, texting, video calls, immersive telepresence, neuro-tech and artificial intelligence all require policymakers and legal systems to grapple with new and frequently untested tools in a relatively short space of time. Novel, and likely cheaper, ways of communicating, gathering data and making decisions are frequently being added to this list of innovations. Rapid acceleration in technological advances is such that futurists are predicting that machines will soon have the computational capacity of the brain and have acquired all human knowledge and proficiencies including pattern recognition powers, problem solving skills, emotional and possibly even moral intelligence (Susskind, 2008). The challenge in deciding which aspects of technology should be embraced, modified, regulated, or rejected is all too clear.

The public sector frequently approaches these challenges in the shadow of developments in the private sector; with technological change commonly being posited as an unavoidable imperative. The rise of platform capitalism brings with it new organisational forms, vast networks of information created and mediated by machines, re-organisation of the world of work and a focus on minimal ownership of physical estates. Against this backdrop, the dominant narrative in advanced capitalist states has become one of change and paradigm shifts (Srnicek, 2017). Though most often discussed in the context of the commercial sphere and the use of AI and big data, this narrative has also impacted the public sphere. Technology is almost always a feature of contemporary large-scale government reforms and is touted as a mechanism for the delivery of greater efficiencies and financial savings.[1] At the same time significant sections of the public, and the business community in particular, increasingly expect the government to make use of technology to streamline the provision of services and keep digital government services open 24 hours a day, seven days a week.[2] Transactions with government departments such as renewing a passport or paying tax online are judged by the calibre of service citizens receive from online banking or online shopping (Benjamin & Potts, 2018).

The authors approach these issues with an open mind, examining the research evidence that is currently available with a view to promoting debate, anticipating impending change and mapping out a future research agenda. Charting this territory involves considering the opposing arguments made by techno-evangelicals, technophobes and trial romantics. A burgeoning body of research, including that produced by the authors, suggests that even when rigorous evaluations of developments are available, a straightforward answer to the questions posed above is no longer straightforward. Developments such as online hearings, in which litigants and others appear in court from their homes, can be seen as rendering justice geographically and metaphorically remote, sterile or even mundane. Viewed from another perspective they are a means through which justice can be brought to the homes of citizens, allowing them to avoid the inconvenient, inhibiting and sometimes degrading experiences of attending a physical court.

The primary perspective from which we have decided to explore these issues is that of the citizen or lay participant in the legal system. While the experiences of judges, court administrators, clerks, ushers, computer engineers, barristers and solicitors remain important, and inform each of the chapters in this book, our approach is essentially a bottom-up one which concentrates on how change is likely to be perceived and experienced by citizens with little legal knowledge. Looking at change and reform from this perspective raises the important issue of who benefits from these transformations, what citizens expect from the modern state and the extent to which historical practices in the delivery of justice are being rendered obsolete.

Responding to technological innovation is particularly demanding for legal systems which have traditionally relied heavily on paper and physical presence. In an English and Welsh context, significant underinvestment in the justice system until recently has also severely limited the agility of the system in implementing the radical changes in thinking and practice now required. One implication of this for the authors is the desire to discuss what technology makes possible, while also having to acknowledge the problems with the actual implementation. Empirical research undertaken by the Law Society (2023) suggests that widespread confusion, variation, fragmentation and lack of trust continue to be barriers to the successful introduction of technological innovation in the justice system. Navigating the chasm between the 'is' and the 'could be' has important implications for the compact between state and citizen in the information age.

In a book of this size, we have inevitably had to make difficult choices about what to include and exclude. This is particularly hard in a field in which technology seems to be impacting all aspects of the civil and criminal justice system. In the interest of offering some in-depth analysis, we have focused on technologically mediated developments in the organisation of trials or hearings and the lead up to them. We have chosen not to delve into online legal advice and education or the use of surveillance and recognition technologies, predictive policing or crime mapping by the police and management of offenders.[3] In addition, we do not take account of the impact of technology on the legal professions, though there is interesting work emerging in this field and this is alluded to in some chapters. Our intention is not to suggest that these are not important areas of inquiry but rather that they are specialist topics in their own right and deserve much more attention than we are able to give them here. Finally, our main focus is on developments in England and Wales. We are aware of the vast amount of literature on what we discuss from around the world and have tried to draw on the most important research produced to date in the chapters that follow. Inevitably there will be some omissions. In the remainder of this chapter, we scope out in more detail the particular issues that we have chosen to focus on. In the course of doing so, we chart the many reasons why a book of this kind is important, and why it is important now.

What Are the Problems Technology Is Meant to Solve? A Brief History of Reform in England and Wales

It has been argued that at first sight, the justice system does not appear to be a good candidate for rapid innovation, characterised as it is by notions of certainty and consistency. Despite this, there has been no shortage of aspirational policy reports outlining the need for the radical reform of the legal system in England and Wales, many of which have advocated the greater use of technology to address the serious shortcomings of twenty-first-century legal systems. Particular attention has been drawn to the fact that the legal system has long depended on outdated and slow paper-based systems, which rely on manual data entry and create inefficiencies, delays, unnecessary costs and a poor experience of the service (Woolf, 1995, 1996; National Audit Office, 2018). Even when technology has been put in place, criticisms have been made of the fact that many of the systems introduced across different courts and tribunals are incapable of sharing information. By way of example, the National Audit Office reported in 2018 that over 70 different legacy systems were in use across the court service.

The modern history of calls for the introduction of a large-scale technological infrastructure can be traced back to the Woolf reports published at the end of the last century.[4] In his final report, Lord Woolf devoted a whole chapter to the subject,[5] recommending that the power of technology should be harnessed in order to improve the performance of the civil justice system with a particular focus on controlling costs and rendering them proportionate to the case (Woolf, 1996). His wide-ranging review, undertaken from 1994–1996, heralded a fundamental rethinking of the UK civil justice process and has been described by Zuckerman (1996) as the most far-reaching review of civil procedure to have been conducted in living memory. Doubt has since been cast on whether the reforms introduced in its wake led to the less adversarial, cheaper, and fairer justice system he called for. However, the significance of his work in the current context is the ways in which it anticipated that technology would not only assist in streamlining and improving existing systems but it would also be a catalyst for more radical change. Re-reading the report makes clear how far society and the civil justice system have come in the time since the Woolf report (1996) was published. References to 'lawyers and judges [who] are reported to be using the Internet' (p. 294) and 'the global information system, known as the WorldWideWeb' which had 'gained enormously in popularity' (p. 287) now appear quaint. But its predictions about the value of video hearings, the importance of customised project management software, and its call for a coherent national infrastructure for the court service and legal profession, are not only of ongoing significance but are also, in some sections of the court service, unrealised.

Enthusiasm for the use of technology to increase efficiency has been equally evident in the field of criminal justice (Royal Commission, 1993; Auld, 2001). In his review of the criminal courts, Lord Justice Auld (2001) called for the government to harness the potential of technology to create a single information technology system for the criminal courts to facilitate case tracking, case management information and the unification of databases; as well as a review of the provision of video link facilities for vulnerable witnesses. Soon after, the Leveson Report (2015) was to suggest that the criminal justice system was crowded with plans for future development. It was this latter report which laid out the most detailed account of the role of technology in realising these plans and building momentum for more radical change in the ways in which different parts of the criminal justice system interacted. In the words of the report:

> The work of the criminal justice system currently relies on a combination of long-standing manual processes and aging computer systems that have evolved in a piecemeal fashion over many decades. There is no doubt that to increase the efficiency of the system, we need better, quicker and less costly ways of creating, filing and distributing documents; easier and more flexible ways of enabling all those involved in the process to communicate effectively with one another. We need to reduce the number of hearings at which the participants have to attend in person. It is critical that we avoid duplication of work […] and that we reduce administrative errors. Well-constructed IT has the potential to overcome most of these challenges. (p. 5–6)

Technological innovation in the criminal justice system has not been without its problems and the government admitted prior to the launch of the recent modernisation programme that substantial sums invested in information technology have been wasted and that the implementation of new technologies has been fragmented (Ministry of Justice, 2012).

A key problem with harnessing technology in the delivery of the justice system has been securing public funds to pay for an adequate infrastructure across the courts and tribunals service. Enthusiasm for change was initially high and the publication by the Lord Chancellor's Department (LCD) of a consultation paper in 1998 reflected excitement about using technology to improve the efficiency of the justice system (Lord Chancellor's Department, 1998). For Susskind (2008), the paper even raised some controversial issues which the Woolf report (1996) had skirted around. These included discussion of whether hearings had to take place in courtrooms, or whether oral evidence is always necessary. Under the enthusiastic leadership of Geoff Hoon, Minister of State for the LCD, a Civil Justice IT Strategy Development Group was established, made up of departmental officials and external members. The group was tasked with the role of capturing and evaluating long-term ideas to inform wider strategic planning[6] and the LCD Strategy paper that followed entitled 'civil.justice.2000' advocated the more extensive use of virtual hearings and electronic case files (Susskind, 2008). However, these initiatives lost momentum and Richard Susskind, who had acted as IT adviser to the Lord Chief Justice, has attributed the lack of investment to two factors. The first of these is the large infrastructure costs required. The second, which reveals much about the government's attitude to change, was fear on the part of the Treasury that the expenditure would not reduce the running costs of the civil justice system but *merely* render it more efficient (Susskind, 2008; see also Fishenden, 2023). The decision not to make the significant investment needed meant that the English and Welsh justice system soon began to lag behind other systems across the world in terms of embracing technology. Notable examples of a more forward-looking approach to investing in technology include Singapore which was an early adopter of e-filing and electronic case management (Magnus, 1999).[7]

In time, the UK Treasury became convinced that a digitised court system would be cheaper to run than a largely paper-based system which was vulnerable during periods of austerity. In 2008 a Ministry of Justice capability review highlighted major performance problems at a time when the Ministry was also having to implement spending cuts. Despite the negative financial environment, leading officials and ministers recognised that there was simply no way that the department could meet its objectives without radical change in the way that it delivered its services (Gash & McCrae, 2010). The result was the Transforming Justice project, a portfolio of activities aimed at achieving a better justice system at less cost to the public. Reflecting on the initiative Gash and McCrae (2010) reported:

> There is a sense of urgency in the department about the need for change, with the leadership unanimously recognising the case for transformation. This has been maintained, and indeed strengthened, with an emphasis on achieving 'better for less' increasing throughout the design phase. (p. 6)

The result was that HM Courts and Tribunals (HMCTS) initiated an ambitious programme of court reform involving an investment of £1.2bn in new technologies in 2016. The reasoning behind the reforms was that financial savings in judicial, administrative, and estate costs would be made by automating processes, selling off outdated parts of the court estate, creating cross-jurisdictional hearing centres, introducing centralised customer service centres, and moving some proceedings online. The National Audit Office has since expressed confidence in the potential of these initiatives to reduce costs. By way of example, it has been anticipated that there will be fewer ineffective and cancelled trials as a result of better information sharing and automation (National Audit Office, 2018, 2023). There have also been a number of back-office transformations of which the most notable is the common platform project, a digital case management system which has been described as a central plank of the reforms (NAO, 2023). If implemented successfully, these various court reform initiatives are expected to deliver annual savings in the region of £220m from 2025–2026 onwards.[8]

The reforms have been self-styled as one of the most ambitious and comprehensive court and tribunal reform programmes in the world.[9] Reflecting on the enormity of the programme, former Lord Chief Justice, Baron Thomas of Cwmgiedd, has argued that they are the most radical to be introduced into the English and Welsh justice system since 1874 (Rozenberg, 2018). An HMCTS-commissioned review of the programme found that the changes involved are far broader than comparable programmes in other countries (NAO, 2019; House of Commons, 2019). Elsewhere, the programme has repeatedly been called ambitious radical or on a scale which has never been attempted in a legal system before (Briggs, 2016; Gash & McCrae, 2010; House of Commons Public Accounts Committee, 2019, 2021b; NAO, 2019, 2023,). Significantly, the reforms have also received the support of senior members of the judiciary. The publication of *Transforming Our Justice System* by the Lord Chancellor, Lord Chief Justice, and the Senior President of Tribunals (2016) talked of combining respected traditions of the legal system with the enabling power of technology and commitment to significant change:

> Every generation has updated or reformed the justice system to adapt to changing times. From the sealing of Magna Carta to the protection of judicial independence in the 1701 Act of Settlement, to the creation of the Crown Court in the 1970s there has never been a moment of stagnation or complacency. (p. 16)

In a similar vein, former Lord Chief Justice, Lord Burnett of Maldon, has argued that judges see the reforms as a 'long-overdue modernisation of our systems' (House of Commons Justice Committee (Reforms, 2019, para 2). Table one summarises some of the projects in the resulting reform portfolio which are most relevant to this book (Table 1.1).[10]

Table 1.1 Major projects included in the HMCTS reform programme[11]

System	Details
Generic changes	
Digital and technology infrastructure[12]	Delivery of Wi-Fi to all courts and tribunals, upgrading Wi-Fi in criminal courts; provision of video hearing and digital evidence hardware, touch screen devices for witnesses and unrepresented litigants to view case materials. and digitisation of paper-based processes
Courts and Tribunal Service Centres	Centralisation of the administration of the courts and tribunals and provision of support to litigants inside and outside of core business hours. Supporting virtual hearings[13]
Scheduling	Scheduling and listing tool called 'ListAssist' to organise when and where hearings will be held including an automated publishing platform that allows information sharing across the criminal, civil, family and tribunal jurisdictions[14]
Common Platform	A single criminal case management system that allows all parties (CPS, HMCTS and professionals) involved in a criminal case to access and share information from charge to conviction.[15] Victims and witnesses will be able to access the system for information on their case
Single system changes	
Adoption procedure	Online service for users including local authorities to manage the legal aspects of adoption cases
Social Security and Child Support	Online service allowing submission, tracking and management of appeals against the DWP decisions
Immigration and asylum	Online system which enables users to manage appeals against Home Office decisions
Divorce and financial remedy	Online system for couples and their legal representative to apply for an uncontested divorce or civil partnership and resolve associated financial issues
Probate	Online service for non-contentious applications for a grant of probate
Family public law	Online service to allow local authorities to complete and submit online applications for childcare and supervision orders for children in need of protection

(continued)

Table 1.1 (continued)

System	Details
Family private law	Online service to allow litigants to initiate and manage cases involving family disputes relating to children
Special Tribunals[16]	Online service to enable and improve data sharing and reduce duplication
Possession claims[17]	Online service which speeds up actions to recover possession of property[18]
Enforcement	Cross jurisdictional service for the enforcement of final judgements, orders, and awards from civil, family and tribunal proceedings
Civil money claims	Online service for the management of civil claims under £10,000
Damages claims	Online service allowing registered legal professionals to issue a claim for damages on behalf of their client
Bulk scanning	Bulk scanning services using character recognition technology to process handwritten forms digitally
Single justice system	Online digital case management systems used by organisations such as the police which facilitates a single Magistrate sitting with a legal adviser can decide low-level, victimless cases such as speeding
Employment tribunals	Online system to manage and present cases
Royal Courts of Justice and Upper Tribunals	Digital case management system bringing together all information relating to a specific civil case

It can be seen from Table One that the programme involves a range of projects across the courts and tribunals service involving digitalisation of document exchange; paperless hearings; and online exchanges between the parties and the judge across the civil and criminal justice estate.[19]

The rhetoric underpinning reform has frequently been presented in terms of greater efficiency (Briggs, 2016; House of Commons Justice Committee Reforms report, 2019a), but two other concepts are worthy of note in this context. The first of these is the claim that the level of resources devoted to the resolution of a dispute needs to be proportionate; freeing up space and time for the most serious of cases. HMCTS intends to do this through increased use of 'remote hearings' and by allowing defendants to enter guilty pleas online rather than holding pre-trial hearings. The aim is to ensure that minor non-custodial offences such as TV licence evasion can be managed completely online.[20] HMCTS aims to reduce the number of criminal cases requiring a physical court hearing each year by around half from 1.7 million to 0.9 million. In the family courts there is a similar plan to reduce the number of cases requiring a physical hearing from 2.6 million to 1 million a year. Elsewhere, specialist case officers will also free up judicial time for contentious issues by undertaking routine 'judicial' tasks in new online systems.[21]

Another purported goal of the reforms is to increase the accessibility of the litigation system by making it more user-friendly for non-lawyers (NAO, 2019). This involves a number of initiatives including a new legal education programme which will alert lay users to their rights and how they can be enforced; digital triage systems which will guide litigants in person through the issues raised by their claim; and a system in which all those involved in the resolution of the case will be able to comment on documents online. It has been argued that these new systems will empower people to negotiate a system at their convenience, using technological tools that they already use in other parts of their lives (Ryder, 2016). Examples of reforms in this category which have already been realised include the new online uncontested probate and divorce systems which aim to allow citizens to lodge and follow the progress of their case online without professional assistance.[22] Other projects said to increase accessibility to services include the five new national Courts & Tribunals Service Centres (CTSCs) using telephone advice, email and webchat to provide a first point of contact for the public (NAO, 2023). Concerns that some users of the court service will find the use of so many online services challenging prompted the launch of a 'digital support service' including face-to-face assistance, initially piloted in partnership with the 'Good Things Foundation', and later taken over by the social impact company 'We Are Digital.' As of December 2022, HMCTS claimed to have received nearly 1,400 referrals for the service, booked appointments with over 900 individuals and helped over 770 users submit an application to one of the new online services.[23]

There are numerous early examples of success in achieving the goals set by the reform programme. HMCTS reported in 2023 that cases submitted digitally through their new online social security and child support service took a third of the time to complete compared to those previously submitted on paper. HMCTS staff are also returning less than one per cent of online divorce applications because of user error, compared to 40% on the paper-based system.[24] A new digital tool for listing court and tribunal hearings has been developed and is now being used in 50,000 cases each week by all civil and family courts. The digital service supporting local authority child welfare cases has also been launched and has been used over 12,000 times.[25] The Common Platform is now live in 173 Crown and magistrates' courts, meaning that 73% of all criminal courts are managing cases on the system (NAO, 2023). Between 1 January 2022 and 30 September 2022, over 530,000 low-level criminal cases were also completed through the new Single Justice Procedure.[26] It would seem that these initiatives have considerable potential to reduce the cost of the legal system to the public purse and render systems much more efficient.

In common with other justice systems across the world, the global Coronavirus pandemic has had a significant impact on the policy landscape and technological developments we seek to critique.[27] Prohibitions on people gathering in the same space meant that thousands, if not millions, of court-based hearings, arbitrations and mediations across continents went online. What was once ordinary became rare and what was once rare became ordinary. Plans to roll out audio and video hearings as part of the reform programme were accelerated and technology naysayers and sceptics were forced to use the very online and digital systems they had been resisting. The impact of the pandemic on the wellbeing of the nation was undoubtedly disastrous but the sudden switch to large-scale machine mediated interactions also served as a social science experiment in which new justice facilities were designed, remote interactions became the norm, digital document exchange was widely practised, and court staff and users were forced to familiarise themselves and experiment with unfamiliar systems.[28] For some, this accelerated change has been seen as a point of no return which will lead to permanent changes in thinking about the possibilities of technology (see for instance Criminal Justice Joint Inspection, 2021; House of Lords Select Committee, 2021; NAO, 2023).

A Neo-Liberal Dream? Difficult Journeys Into Uncharted Waters

The discourse surrounding the reforms and the logic of efficiency, proportionality and modernity are compelling but is also important to place them in the context of long-standing academic critiques of attempts on the part of the government to reduce the number of people gaining access to high-quality justice (see for instance Abel, 1982; Genn, 1999). Frequently associated with the notion of new public management concepts drawn from the private sector, this language raises concerns about the ways in which the citizen–state relationship is recast into a series of customer-provider transactions which focus on the needs of the system at the expense of public services. For Fishenden (2023) this undermines the true potential of digital transformation to rebuild and redesign the public sector around a more democratic and effective citizen–state relationship which encourages engagement in policy-making between elections and increases transparency and trust.

Despite the rhetoric around the reform programme, it is important to note that it is an overall decline in commitment to the legal system which is fuelling many of the changes outlined above. In 2019–2020 the total Ministry of Justice budget was around 25% lower than in 2010–2011 (House of Commons, 2019) and it could be argued that as a result, the government has created many of the problems it is now seeking to solve. One of the reasons why initiatives such as online legal education, advice, triaging of cases, and video hearings can be presented as attractive is the lacuna caused by the severe reduction of the provision of legal aid after the Legal Aid, Sentencing and Punishment of Offenders Act 2012 and the historic underfunding of the advice sector.[29] Under provision of legal services is reflected in increasing recognition of the presence of 'advice deserts' across the UK in which there are few, if any, locally based providers of legal aid and advice services. Recent research undertaken by Wintersteiger et al. (2021) for the Legal Service Board claimed that 3.6 million adults a year have an unmet legal need involving a dispute.[30] In a similar vein, work undertaken by the Law Society (2023) in mapping the location of practitioners who can provide legally aided advice demonstrates that 25.3 million people in England and Wales do not have access to face-to-face housing advice from lawyers and that existing provision in the field of community care, education and welfare advice was in decline.[31] These problems are particularly severe for disadvantaged groups living in rural communities with weak transport infrastructure.

In his review of civil justice Lord Justice Briggs (2016) acknowledged that the reduction in legal aid had played a role in creating the problems of an under-utilised estate that HMCTS then 'solved' by closing down courts (see also NAO, 2019). In short, it was a problem of under-provision which enabled HMCTS to close 127 courts on the basis that they would be providing more flexible court buildings or 'hearing centres', with better facilities and technology to facilitate digital working (House of Commons Public Accounts Committee, 2019b). Particular disquiet has arisen in relation to the inaccessibility of remaining courts for those with disabilities, on a low income, or living in rural area where public transport systems are less regular and more expensive (House of Commons, 2019b). It has also become a cause for concern that to date HMCTS has failed to produce a formal evaluation of the impact of court closures.

There is also a danger that the discussion of the radical nature of the reforms recently introduced has been overstated or pays insufficient attention to the paucity of previous investment. The English and Welsh legal system has been a late adopter in creating a technological infrastructure for the courts when compared to other developed nations. At the beginning of the reforms the system was still operating with locally developed and outdated processes. This created a testing operational environment in which to innovate. Not only was the estate run down, but there were also long backlogs in some parts of the system and recruiting judges in some jurisdictions was proving hard (NAO, 2023). This frequently meant that the baseline for improvement was also extremely low. Pre-reform technological developments have been described as 'antiquated' and 'virtually below sea level' (House of Lords 2021, Chapter 2, Para 37) and in a parlous state (Susskind, 2008). Speaking in 2018, Lord Burnett concluded that the pre-reform programme courts sat 'in splendid technological isolation, unable to talk to each other or anyone in the outside world' (Lord Justice Burnett, 2018). As a result, rather than implementing radical and ambitious new systems, much of the reform programme has been focused on installing basic 'plumbing' such as compatible networked

PCs, secure intranet sites, and email networks for judges, administrators and lawyers.

Despite these successes, the English and Welsh case study makes obvious the challenges of reform on the scale outlined above. While many of the aims of the court reform programme are laudable, it has been repeatedly suggested that the programme is too ambitious. Particular attention has been paid to the fact that it has involved multiple projects designed to create new technology from scratch involving a diverse group of users based in different pockets of the civil, criminal, tribunal, and family court systems, each of which has their own unique cultures with no 'single owner' (NAO, 2019). One result of these challenges is that HMCTS has struggled to deliver all they promised in the timetable set out (NAO, 2019) or to deliver the savings promised (NAO, 2023). The launch of several projects has now been delayed including the rollout of the common platform[32] To date, this has led to three extensions of the timetable for delivering the court reform programme (NAO, 2023).

The concept of proportionality is also troubling in this context. Dispute resolution specialists have long argued for the need to fit the forum to the fuss (Goldberg & Sander, 1994), and it is questionable that the general public would want to pay for TV licence evaders to attend a court even if resources were unlimited. But the language of proportionality suggests that it is easy for us to decide what cases are 'important' and more deserving of State resources. By way of example, one of the questionable principles underpinning the introduction of litigation tracks in the English and Welsh civil justice system has been that the level of damages claimed is indicative of the importance of the issues which need to be resolved. This assumption ignores the importance of small amounts of damages to those on low incomes or the value of points of law which might arise in 'small' or minor pieces of litigation (Mulcahy, 2013). Viewed in this way the concept of proportionality can very easily become code for the State deciding that small cases or those involving the disadvantaged are not considered important by the legal elite. It is interesting to note, for instance, how many of the new systems outlined in Table One focus on digitalisation of systems relating to debt, social security and family disputes.

In addition to economic concerns, political, social and philosophical questions about the sort of justice we want need to be urgently addressed. The pandemic undoubtedly created conditions in which techno-sceptics became more familiar with the possibilities of technology, but important questions also began to be asked about whether it is appropriate to use remote hearings in all cases or to compel those with low-value claims to engage online (Byrom et al., 2020; Criminal Justice Joint Inspection, 2021; Ryan et al., 2020). The incidence and causes of digital disadvantage and the digital divide also came into sharp relief during the pandemic, giving rise to concerns about those who were being left behind by the reform programme, which is in danger of creating, or re-enforcing a two-tier justice system. A particular problem which has emerged is the lack of in-depth quality research into the impact of the reforms. In the words of the House of Commons Public Accounts Committee 2019b:

It remains unclear how the reforms are affecting access to justice, especially for vulnerable people. HMCTS has not shown it is doing enough to understand the impact on court and tribunal users before pressing ahead with reforms, increasing the risk that justice outcomes might be affected, particularly with the court closure programme. (p. 3)

In a similar vein, the Justice Committee in 2019 has talked of a dearth of concrete empirical evidence about the performance of technologies and a surfeit of sophisticated speculation (see also National Audit Office, 2023; Law Society, 2023). This is particularly the case as regards vulnerable users of the legal system who can be difficult to reach and engage in research (Mulcahy & Tsalapatanis, 2022). One result of this is widespread concern about the likelihood that technological innovation is not being tailored to the needs of all citizens (House of Commons Justice Committee, 2020). As this book goes to press the recommendation of the House of Commons Select Committee on Justice made in 2020, continues to have resonance:

...work must be done urgently to identify the effects of increased use of digital technology for the delivery of justice not only on the process and disposal of cases but on the results obtained for those whose cases and hearings have taken place; their perception on the fairness of the proceedings, regardless of outcome; and the barriers to access and understanding that may have arisen for both participants in cases and the wider public, including the media. (p. 5)

Their assertion that changes introduced during the pandemic should not be regarded as irreversible if they can be shown to impede access to justice remains a challenge to all of us interested in access to justice.

Organisation of this Book

Several features distinguish this monograph. Firstly, it adopts a multi-disciplinary socio-legal perspective which will draw on scholarly insights from across the social sciences including law, sociology, science and technology studies and legal geography. There is a particular focus on the emerging body of empirical evidence about the phenomenology of online services and hearings. Secondly, the issues raised have a global significance. In the UK and beyond, governments are making increasing use of technology. As a result, the book draws on scholarship about online hearings from a number of jurisdictions including, the Netherlands, Australia, Canada and the US while maintaining a primary focus on England and Wales as a case study. Thirdly, the book aims to be accessible and provocative; attempting to disrupt the entrenched positions on the topic which are frequently apparent from existing debate.

Following this introduction, Chapter Two explores what we mean by digital justice and tries to make sense of the many ways in which technology is now mediating processes and relationships in the justice system. Focusing on civil justice, it draws on examples from around the world, examining the extent to which technology is being used to just substitute paper for digital or transforming the essential nature of how we interact.

Chapter Three considers the benefits of online justice. It argues that moving justice online not only offers the chance to make justice systems more efficient and accessible but provides the opportunity to reimagine how we facilitate greater participation between citizens and the state. The chapter will contend that there is an urgent need to move away from romanticised accounts of the courtroom as pseudo-scared spaces, which socio-legal accounts of courtroom dynamics and legal process have frequently been found to be false. While remaining sceptical about the claims of techno-evangelicals, it considers how new technologies can remake the spatial and temporal world of the justice system with a view to greater accessibility and sensitivity to the needs of the disadvantaged.

Chapter Four considers what is lost when justice moves online. More specifically it addresses the ways in which legal hearings have traditionally been synonymous with special places, collective ceremonies, rituals, and materiality. The implications of this will be explored in relation to the significance of co-presence, the engendering of a sense of civic occasion, the exercise of State power and its impact on the sensory and psychological quality of interactions. It will reflect on what is lost when the courtroom or hearing room becomes dispersed or transformed into a series of mundane private spaces which people arrive at, and depart from, at the click of a button. The chapter makes two arguments. Firstly, the arrival of online justice heralds a retreat of the State from the civic sphere. Secondly, the shift primarily serves those with political, cultural and social capital and renders more intense the divide between the digitally empowered and the left behind.

The final chapter raises a number of epistemological issues about different ways of seeing the justice system. Focusing on the needs of the most disadvantaged users of the legal system we ask a series of questions about the ways in which the mindset of current architects of online justice systems and content providers can be seen as biased. The chapter argues that this is due in large part to a failure to take into account the needs and opinions of public users of the justice system in the design, testing and implementation of online services. Drawing on concepts of participatory design we outline the various ways in which the creation of new knowledge through interacting with the general public constitutes a form of democratic and responsible design.

Notes

1. The launch of the UK Government Digital Service in 2011 is a prime example of this. Set up as a unit of the Cabinet Office it is tasked with transforming the provision of online public services and implementing

the government's 'Digital by Default' strategy. For strategies developed in other jurisdictions see further: US—https://18f.gsa.gov/what-we-deliver/; Australia—https://www.dta.gov.au/; Canada—https://digital.canada.ca/, last accessed July 2023.
2. In the UK, responsibility for improving government's performance rests with the Central Digital and Data Office and the Government Digital Service which are both part of the Cabinet Office. Individual departments are responsible for the day-to-day delivery of their own programmes (House of Commons Public Accounts Committee, 2021).
3. For a discussion of these issues see Byrne and Marx, 2011; Foster, 2005; Moriarty, 2005, Ernst et al., 2021. Debate in this field raises a host of really important questions about the acquisition and use of data and the implications of this for responsible innovation and civil liberties.
4. The use of technology in the legal system can be traced back to the advent of the telephone and computer assisted transcription. Under the JUDITH project, introduced prior to the Woolf reforms, a number of judges were supplied with personal computers linked to the judicial communications network known as FELIX (Woolf, 1996). However, it was the Woolf reports which really made the case for a strategic approach to the provision of infrastructure.
5. See also chapter 13 of the interim report (Woolf, 1995).
6. Civil Justice IT Strategy Development Group: https://www.scl.org/articles/288-civil-justice-it-strategy-development-group
7. See also the Courtroom 21 project set up in the US with a view to experimenting with the use of technology in the courtroom.
8. The expected savings from the programme have since decreased. The programme's expected lifetime savings are now £2 billion, £310 million (13%) less than in 2019 (NAO, 2023).
9. https://insidehmcts.blog.gov.uk/2023/03/20/hmcts-reform-achievements-challenges-and-next-steps/; https://www.gov.uk/guidance/the-hmcts-reform-programme#what-weve-achieved. On this point see also Byrom, (2019); Susskind (2019).
10. Other reforms not noted in the chart aim to provide the infrastructure and workforce to support the improved system.
11. Appendix 2 NAO (2023) was a major source of information in the compilation of this table.
12. See further: https://www.gov.uk/guidance/hmcts-video-hearings-service-guidance-for-joining-a-hearing. In 2023 HMCTS announced that over 70% of all courtrooms, including over 90% of Crown courtrooms, can now allow parties in a case to join hearings remotely, where deemed appropriate by the judiciary: https://www.gov.uk/guidance/the-hmcts-reform-programme#what-weve-achieved
13. See further: https://hmctsjobs.co.uk/roles/national-services-court-tribunal-service-centres-ctsc-national-business-centres-nbc/

14. See further: https://www.gov.uk/guidance/hmcts-services-scheduling-and-listing-project
15. This is now live in 76% of criminal courts: https://insidehmcts.blog.gov.uk/2023/03/20/hmcts-reform-achievements-challenges-and-next-steps/, Last visited July 2023.
16. Special tribunals are a set of ten tribunals such as the Mental Health Property and Special Educational Needs and Disability Tribunals.
17. As of July 2023 work on the Special Tribunals and Possession systems was paused: https://insidehmcts.blog.gov.uk/2023/03/20/hmcts-reform-achievements-challenges-and-next-steps/
18. See further: https://www.possessionclaim.gov.uk/pcol/
19. An investment of £270 million in digitalisation of criminal justice system announced in 2015.
20. By way of example, for low-level offences such as vehicle offences, those who plead guilty online can receive their sentence immediately rather than wait for an available hearing date.
21. https://insidehmcts.blog.gov.uk/2023/03/20/hmcts-reform-achievements-challenges-and-next-steps/
22. See further: https://www.gov.uk/divorce/file-for-divorce
23. https://www.gov.uk/government/publications/hmcts-reform-infrastructure-and-enabling-services-fact-sheets/fact-sheet-national-digital-support-service
24. See further https://insidehmcts.blog.gov.uk/2023/03/20/hmcts-reform-achievements-challenges-and-next-steps/
25. https://www.gov.uk/guidance/the-hmcts-reform-programme#what-weve-achieved
26. HMCTS June 2023: https://www.gov.uk/guidance/the-hmcts-reform-programme#what-weve-achieved.
27. Use of technology in justice systems increased even in those countries such as Nigeria where the infrastructure was inadequate, there was poor bandwidth and irregular power supply.
28. In a UK context HMCTS received an additional £150 m in Government funding to respond to the COVID-19 pandemic which was intended to fund new technology to enable remote hearings; additional temporary courtrooms big enough to facilitate social distancing which became known in the UK as 'Nightingale courtrooms'; personal protective equipment and additional staff. See also the statutory provisions contained in The Coronavirus Act 2020 and The Criminal Procedure (Amendment No. 2) (Coronavirus) Rules 2020 (2020 No. 417 [L. 12]); and The Civil Procedure (Amendment No. 2) (Coronavirus) Rules 2020 (2020 No. 582 [L. 13]).
29. This Act had a dramatic impact on the availability of legal aid in England and Wales with the result that legal aid is now unobtainable for a wide range of civil cases. The Law Society (2023) has claimed that together with cuts in local authority funding this has caused half the

law centres in England and Wales offering free legal advice to be shut down. A recent report by The Community Justice Fund suggests that nearly 43,000 people will be unable to get specialist and legal advice in 2023–2024 and that the sector faces a funding deficit amounting to over £32million. See further: https://nfj.org.uk/wp-content/uploads/2021/10/2023-Funding-Gap-Report-FINAL.pdf

30. The report describes public legal education as equipping people with the awareness, knowledge and understanding of rights and legal issues together with the confidence and skills they need to deal with disputes and gain access to justice.
31. https://www.lawsociety.org.uk/campaigns/civil-justice/legal-aid-deserts
32. These included issues such as lagging and slow system responses that interfered with the live-running of courts. HMCTS and CPS found replacing existing legacy systems with a modernised single system and managing large projects in an agile way was more challenging than they first expected (NAO, 2023).

Bibliography

Abel, R. (1982). The Politics of Informal Justice. In *The Politics of Informal Justice: The American experience*. New York: Academic Press.

Auld, Lord Justice. (2001). *Review of the Criminal Courts of England and Wales*. https://www.criminal-courts-review.org.uk/auldconts.htm

Benjamin, K., & Potts, H. W. (2018). Digital Transformation in Government: Lessons for Digital Health? *Digital Health, 3*, 1–5.

Briggs, L. J. (2016). *Civil Courts Structure Review: Final Report by Lord Justice Briggs*. https://www.judiciary.uk/wp-content/uploads/2016/07/civil-courts-structure-review-final-report-jul-16-final-1.pdf

Byrom, N., Beardon, S., & Kendrick, A. (2020). *The Impact of COVID-19 Measures on the Civil Justice System*, Civil Justice Council and legal Education Foundation. https://www.judiciary.uk/wp-content/uploads/2020/06/CJC-Rapid-Review-Final-Report-f.pdf

Byrne, J., & Marx, G. (2011). Technological Innovations in Crime Prevention and Policing: A Review of Research on Implementation and Impact. *Journal of Police Studies, 3*(20), 17–40.

Criminal Justice Joint Inspection. (2021). *Impact of the Pandemic on the Criminal Justice System A Joint view of the Criminal Justice Chief Inspectors on the Criminal Justice System's Response to COVID-19*. https://www.justiceinspectorates.gov.uk/cjji/wp-content/uploads/sites/2/2021/01/2021-01-13-State-of-nation_AccessibleVersion.pdf

Ernst, S., ter Veen, H., & Kop, N. (2021). Technological Innovation in a Police Organisation: Lessons Learned from the National Police of the Netherlands. *Policing, 15*(3), 1818–1831.

Fishenden, J. (2023). *Fracture: The Collision Between Technology and Democracy and How We Fix It*. Amazon.

Foster, R. (2005). *Police Technology*. Prentice Hall.
Gash, T., & McCrae, J. (2010). *Transformation in the Ministry of Justice—Interim Evaluation Report*, Institute for Government. https://www.instituteforgovernment.org.uk/sites/default/files/publications/Transformation%20in%20the%20Ministry%20of%20Justice%201st%20Interim%20Report.pdf
Genn, H. (1999). *Paths to Justice: What People Do and Think About Going to Law*. Bloomsbury Publishing.
Goldberg, S., & Sander, F. (1994). Fitting the Forum to the Fuss. *Negotiation Journal, 10*(1).
House of Commons. (2019). *The Spending of the Ministry of Justice*, Debate Pack Number CDP-2019-0217. https://researchbriefings.files.parliament.uk/documents/CDP-2019-0217/CDP-2019-0217.pdf
House of Commons Justice Committee. (2019). *Court and Tribunal Reforms Second Report of Session 2019*, Report, Together with Formal Minutes Relating to the Report Ordered to be printed 30 October 2019 HC 190. https://publications.parliament.uk/pa/cm201919/cmselect/cmjust/190/190.pdf
House of Commons Justice Committee. (2020). *Coronavirus (COVID-19) the Impact on Courts*, Sixth Report of Session 2019–2021, HC 519. https://committees.parliament.uk/publications/2188/documents/20351/default/
House of Commons Public Accounts Committee. (2019a). *Transforming Courts and Tribunals: Progress Review*, Second Report of Session 2019 Report, Together with Formal Minutes Relating to the Report Ordered by the House of Commons to be printed 4 November 2019 HC 27.
House of Commons Public Accounts Committee. (2019b). *Transforming Courts and Tribunals: progress review*, Second Report of Session Report, together with formal minutes relating to the report Ordered to be printed 4 November 2019 HC 27.
House of Commons Public Accounts Committee. (2021a). *Challenges in Implementing Digital Change*, Thirtieth Report of Session 2021–22, HC 637.
House of Lords Select Committee on the Constitution. (2021). *COVID-19 and the Courts 22nd Report of Session 2019–2021*, HL Paper 257.
Law Society. (2023). *Legal Aid Deserts*. https://www.lawsociety.org.uk/campaigns/civil-justice/legal-aid-deserts
Lord Burnett of Maldon, Lord Chief Justice of England and Wales. (2018, June 2). *The Age of Reform: Sir Henry Brooke Annual Lecture*. https://www.judiciary.uk/wp-content/uploads/2018/06/speech-lcj-the-age-of-reform2.pdf
Lord Chancellor, the Lord Chief Justice and the Senior President of Tribunals. (2016). *Transforming Our Justice System*. https://assets.publishing.service.gov.uk/government/uploads/system/uploads/attachment_data/file/553261/joint-vision-statement.pdf
Lord Chancellor's Department. (1998). Civil Justice: *Resolving and Avoiding Disputes in the Information Age*, A consultation paper.
Lord Chancellor's Department. (2000). *Civil.Justice.2000, A Vision of the Civil Justice System in the Information Age: A Strategy Paper*.
Magnus, R. (1999). *E-Justice: The Singapore Story*. Paper presented at the Sixth National Court Technology Conference for the National Centre for State Courts. https://ncsc.contentdm.oclc.org/digital/api/collection/tech/id/642/download
Ministry of Justice. (2012). *Swift and Sure Justice: The Government's Plans for the Reform of the Criminal Justice System*. Ministry of Justice. https://assets.publishing.service.gov.uk/media/5a7ca43a40f0b65b3de0a38e/swift-and-sure-justice.pdf

Moriarty, L. (Ed.). (2005). *Criminal Justice Technology in the 21st Century*. Thomas.

Mulcahy, L. (2013). The Collective Interest in Private Dispute Resolution. *Oxford Journal of Legal Studies, 33*(1), 59–80.

Mulcahy, L., & Tsalapatanis, A. (2022). Exclusion in the Interests of Inclusion: Who Should Stay Offline in the Emerging World of Online Justice? *Journal of Social Welfare and Family Law, 44*(4), 455–476. https://doi.org/10.1080/09649069.2022.2136713

National Audit Office. (2018). *Early Progress in Transforming Courts and Tribunals* HC 1001.

National Audit Office. (2019). *The Challenges in Implementing Digital Change*, HC 575.

National Audit Office. (2023). *Progress on the Courts and Tribunals Reform Programme*, HC 1130.

Royal Commission on Criminal Justice. (1993). Chaired by Viscount Runciman, Cmnd 2263.

Rozenberg, J., 2018, Justice Online: Are We There Yet? Lecture Given at Gresham College London. Available https://www.youtube.com/watch?v=ktjRsvhVpCQ

Ryan, M., Harker, L., & Rothera, S. (2020). *Remote Hearings in the Family Justice System: A Rapid Consultation*. Nuffield Family Justice Observatory.

Ryder, E. (2016, March 3). *5th Annual Ryder Lecture: The University of Bolton. 'The Modernisation of Access to Justice in Times of Austerity'*. https://www.judiciary.uk/wp-content/uploads/2016/03/20160303-ryder-lecture2.pdf

Srnicek, N. (2017). *Platform Capitalism*. Polity Press.

Susskind, R. (2008). *The End of Lawyers*. Oxford University Press.

Susskind, R. (2019). *Online Courts and the Future of Justice*. Oxford University Press.

Wintersteiger, L., Morse, S., Olatokun M., & Morris, C. J. (2021). *Effectiveness of Public Legal Education Initiatives a Literature Review*. London: The Legal Services Board. https://www.legalservicesboard.org.uk/wp-content/uploads/2021/02/PLE-systematic-review-report-Feb-2021.pdf

Woolf, H. (1995). *Access to Justice: Interim Report to the Lord Chancellor on the Civil Justice System in England and Wales*. Lord Chancellors Department.

Woolf, H. (1996). *Final Report to the Lord Chancellor on the Civil Justice System in England and Wales*. London: HMSO.

Zuckerman, A. A. (1996). Lord Woolf's Access to Justice: Plus ça Change. *The Modern Law Review, 59*(6), 773–796.

CHAPTER 2

What Do We Mean by Technological Innovation in the Justice System?

Abstract This chapter explores what we mean by digital justice and tries to make sense of the diverse ways technology is now mediating processes and relationships in justice systems. Using civil justice as a case study and drawing on examples from around the world, it focuses on whether technology is primarily being used to substitute paper and other in-person processes for digital or going further to transform the essential nature of how we interact. More particularly it looks at the ways in which digital files are replacing paper and machines are replacing humans.

Keywords Online dispute resolution · Digitalisation · Artificial intelligence · Platforms · Technology

INTRODUCTION

Discussion of the many ways in which technology is being used in the legal system employs a considerable range of terms such as digitisation, digitalisation, cyberjustice, online dispute resolution (ODR), virtual justice, videolinks, remote hearings and online justice. A plethora of different technologies, systems and processes underlie this vocabulary. Some of them do little more than render the litigation system paperless, but discussion is increasingly focused on how technology allows us to go beyond transforming *how* things are done, to alter *what* is done. This chapter seeks to unravel the innovations possible through the use of such technology, the shifts in ways of thinking they entail, and the ways in which future developments are now being imagined. The compact style of this publication means that this can be no more than

© The Author(s), under exclusive license to Springer Nature Switzerland AG 2024
L. Mulcahy and A. Tsalapatanis, *Digital Justice*, Palgrave Socio-Legal Studies, https://doi.org/10.1007/978-3-031-65265-3_2

an outline and introduction to the issues raised in subsequent chapters. The literature in the area is extensive, growing at a fast pace, increasingly multi-disciplinary and produced from jurisdictions across the world. As a result, the examples chosen are indicative rather than exhaustive.

In the first section of this chapter, we present a typology that involves three ways of thinking about innovation, using the civil justice system as a case study. The first of these is 'as if' technology. The second is enhanced communication and engagement. The third is the replacement of people in the legal system. As we move from the first category to the last we move into the realm of predictions about what is possible in the future rather than what is being practised. We begin with a discussion of changes that are just substitutes for existing systems rather than more broadly transformative, but it becomes clear that all the developments described are disruptive in some way. It will also become apparent that what are frequently framed as technological or procedural issues also have a social and political dimension which we will go on to discuss in subsequent chapters.

Towards a Typology of Technological Developments in the Civil Justice System

Those using justice systems engage in numerous tasks at different stages of the process which can lead up to a hearing. These can be usefully separated out for the purposes of thinking about where most activity occurs in the legal system and how technological innovations can have value. The core stages that people traverse, from identification of a claim to closure, are identified in Fig. 2.1. As the parties progress through the civil justice systems they will be required to engage in a series of tasks that involve alerting the justice system to their claim, articulating the outcome they want, providing evidence, assessing the validity of evidence provided by the other side, narrowing down the issues in dispute, and engaging with the other side and the adjudicator assigned to manage and hear their case. Technological innovation takes many different forms across this process.

Figure 2.1 presents the civil legal process as ending in adjudication, though in reality many claims will be abandoned or settled as a result of bi-lateral negotiations at any stage of the process. This fact may well encourage policy-makers to prioritise digital transformation in the busiest parts of the system. Depending on the nature of the issues in dispute and resources available, many users of the legal system will also progress along the stages shown without a

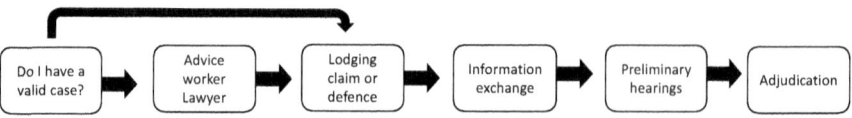

Fig. 2.1 The key stages of the court and tribunal-based dispute resolution

lawyer or adviser as litigants in person become a feature of civil justice. This may have an impact on the ways in which content is written and presented.

Not all of the activity outlined in Fig. 2.1 will involve the court service, meaning that technological innovation may be led from the outside. The process of determining whether you have a valid case or defence will frequently involve private consultations with advice sector workers or lawyers or independent web-based research. Disputants may also opt to have their case determined by a privately appointed arbitrator rather than a state-appointed judge, as is common in the management of large-scale commercial cases and consumer cases involving goods and services. In large-scale commercial cases, well-informed litigants will be keen for the lawyers they instruct to use technology if it results in cost savings. This is one reason why there is so much interest in AI in the sifting and organisation of large amounts of textual evidence. It is significant in this context, that many examples of the most advanced technological solutions come from the private sector, with much attention paid to the ways in which large international e-businesses such as eBay and Amazon have revolutionised the management of low-value high-volume disputes.

Breaking down tasks and steps in this way is significant because it begins to make clear that the drivers of innovation may come from inside and outside of the legal system and that the legal system may be more technologically sophisticated in some places rather than others. With this context in mind, we turn in the remainder of this section to look at the different uses to which technology is being put in the advice sector, the legal system and private dispute resolution forums. Rather than focusing on the sophistication of the technologies involved, we have chosen to concentrate on what the technologies aim to do and the extent to which they challenge traditional ways of thinking about legal systems.

As If Technology

The first cluster of technological innovations can be understood as a set of 'as if' transformations that involve converting what was previously physical into digital format. This process of digitisation includes a range of activities such as replacing legal advice leaflets and posters with online legal education materials; substituting courthouses with online hearings, replacing people with holograms and avatars, or simply changing paper forms into electronic ones. In this section, we discuss the ways in which these innovations are being used at each of the stages outlined in Fig. 2.1.

Starting with the provision of advice, there has been considerable interest in the ways in which access to justice can be improved through the provision of clear guidance on people's rights and how they can be enforced. Innovations in this vein have taken the form of free provision of electronic legal resources such as the British and Irish Legal Information Institute (BAILII), a non-profit making charitable trust, that provides a web-based interactive database of full text primary legal materials without charge or the EU e-justice portal which provides open access to legislation case law and legal information.[1] In a similar vein in Canada, the Public Legal Education and Information Network initiated in 1992 provides an online library of materials, and an online platform for the community of people responsible for justice-related services to meet electronically with a view to fostering collaboration (Gander, 2002). In a UK context, the Citizens Advice website provides a range of useful pages on such issues as managing debt and rent arrears which replaces the traditional reliance of people on lawyers or face-to-face contact with advice agencies. Going one step further, the UK government has introduced an online webchat service which allows people using the Social Security and Child Support Tribunal or the Probate service instant advice from a human adviser.[2]

Technology also has the potential to reduce the inefficiency of initiating a claim or defence without having to produce hard copies of a document that need to be filed at particular places at specific times. Legal systems have traditionally been documented and labour-intensive systems that have had to create, receive, review, index, process, circulate and store large amounts of paper including claims, counter claims, evidence, and documents relating to costs (Susskind, 2008). In the US, Federal and State Courts have been experimenting with e-filing of documents since the early 2000s (Koshykar, 2004; Krause, 2006; Menashe, 2017) and in the UK, a new electronic filing and case management system has been used in the Chancery Division, the Technology and Construction Court, the Admiralty and Commercial Court, and in Bankruptcy and Companies hearings since 2014. This allows for a range of paperless documents to be lodged and sealed by the court.[3] Elsewhere in the legal system, vehicle offences and disputes about penalty notices for parking violations are now being dealt with online from beginning to end (Mulcahy, 2024; National Audit Office, 2019). The *Money Claim Online* system is also being used to lodge claims of up to £10,000 in England and Wales.[4] In Europe the e-Curia systems developed by the European Union allow the parties to exchange procedural documents with Registries by electronic means and the e-CODEX system simplifies cross-border civil and criminal proceedings by providing electronic delivery services, signatures, payment systems and authentication.

The shift from in-person hearings to online hearings involves a more dramatic 'as if' change in how justice is delivered. This transformation can take two forms. The first involves hybrid hearings where some people join an otherwise in-person hearing by videolink. By way of example 'videolinks' have been used to allow vulnerable witnesses to appear in court via a remote connection since the 1990s. Rather than being mere instances of 'as if' technology it could be argued that this practice actually facilitated trials going ahead which might never have taken place if a witness had been compelled to appear in the same room as the person they have accused. Another instance in which most people gather at a hearing centre but others join online involves the use of international experts in commercial cases. The second form of online hearings involves everyone joining a hearing from a different location online. It has been suggested that the move to completely online trials, marks the dematerialisation of the courtroom (Olugasa & Davies, 2022). However, it is probably more accurate to describe this transition as creating a 'distributed' courtroom in which everyone is physically dispersed but present in different material locations (Tait et al., 2017).

Other technological developments that fall under this category include holographic and evidence presentation technology.[5] While not yet common practice, holograms have been used during a mock trial at the Center for Legal and Court Technology where they were considered by some to be superior to seeing someone on screen (Sloan, 2023).[6] Technology experts have argued that augmented reality technology of this kind could, for example, be of value in a product liability case. Equipment at the heart of a case could be represented in 3D format, allowing the judge and others to examine it from every angle.[7] Brought together these developments can be seen as examples of 'electronic courtrooms' that try to replicate the dynamics of an in-person hearing. There are few courts in the world that are fully equipped to deliver all the developments described, though there are a number of university-based experimental courts where technological possibilities of this kind are being tested out. These include the Cyberjustice lab in Montreal and the Center for Legal and Court Technology at William and Mary Law School in Virginia.

At the beginning of this chapter, it was suggested that such uses of technology can be seen as mere substitutes for objects, people and rooms, but we argue that *all* technological innovation is disruptive in some sense. By way of example, systems of the kind discussed above are altering traditional notions of legal time and the rhythm of litigation. Lawyers, judges and lay participants are no longer anchored to one location or in-person interactions, as the lodging and receipt of e-documents take place outside of court hours and relentless connectivity becomes a reality. Concepts of legal place are also being disrupted as courthouses no longer have need of space for extensive filing, registries or hearing rooms. Electronic information highways render the journey of documents around legal space, so eloquently charted by Latour (2010), obsolete as the file and 'the bundle' take on an ephemeral character. These innovations are also having an impact on who is involved in the legal system and the value attached to their labour. Reforms of the kind discussed in this section allow the courts to save on the number of people needed to mail, stamp and handle documents and move them around (Krause, 2006). But, as we will see in the next two sections, technology also has the potential to impact the work of elite workers in the legal system.

Enhanced Communication and Engagement

Moving beyond the goals of 'as if' initiatives, there is an increasing interest in using technology to change the ways in which people interact with state legal systems and other disputants. In this context, technology is being harnessed to provide greater transparency about what is required of people, aiding in the formulation of relevant information, allowing people to track the progress of their claim and facilitating more spontaneous information flows. The shift towards platform provision of state legal services means that they are no longer reliant on email to submit documentation to the court, tribunal or other side or 'flat' web 'pages' that need constant updating and present one-way information. Instead, technology is making possible more dynamic database-driven resources that can customise responses and provide repositories and communication channels not previously accessible to litigants. In his review of the civil court structure in 2016, Lord Justice Briggs explained the process in the following way:

> My study of comparable systems here and abroad suggests that the design and ongoing maintenance of stage 1 of the Online Court is not solely, or even mainly, an IT challenge. It is primarily an exercise in knowledge engineering it requires the construction of a series of questions for litigants (in the form of a decision tree for each case type) which will extract from them the alleged facts and evidence about their case which the court will need to know in determining it (and to which the opposing party will need to be able to respond) […] it will require the questions to be framed in non-legal language. (p. 49)

Platforms of this kind frequently offer lay users of the justice system greater autonomy over the management of their case through dashboards which can be used to track the progress of their case, upload documents and comment on the evidence submitted by other parties. Unlike electronic filing which often involves the submission of documents into a void, dashboards allow users to view all the information submitted to date and the progress of the case. In addition to helping with the phrasing of submissions, these systems frequently allow for both synchronised and asynchronous exchanges between the parties using email or in-system messaging programmes. They also allow for a wide range of materials such as maps, photographs, data, and graphs to be uploaded to a secure and confidential space which both parties can access at a time that is convenient to them. Perhaps most importantly, they support the constant flow of information between the parties in ways that support the correcting of incorrect information, facilitate the exchange of new information and re-assessment of the merits of claim and defence.

Cyber-negotiation tools use some of the same methods in helping to achieve a settlement where there is an impasse between the parties. This form of negotiation can employ technology to help set an agenda for settlement negotiations, suggest solutions that have worked in other similar cases, or allow automated information sharing in which the parties reveal remedies or the level of damage that would be acceptable to them. The *Rechtwijzer* system developed by the Dutch Legal Aid Board provides users with action-oriented information on the steps they can take to resolve their legal problems and can offer referrals to agencies that can provide immediate assistance to those in need. Importantly, the platform uses algorithms to find points of agreement, and then proposes solutions. [8]Cybersettle is another system in this mould that uses a patented, double-blind bidding process focused exclusively on the financial settlement. This allows each side of a dispute to submit the highest and lowest blind bid that would be an acceptable settlement to them. The figures are not disclosed to the other side, but if the machine detects that settlement ranges identified by each of the parties in dispute overlap the final figure is split down the middle. If there is no overlap in the amounts suggested, then the process can be repeated. The system is mainly used by lawyers and claims managers for insurance and personal injury claims where there are no unresolved liability issues and nuisance value has been established.[9] These various examples make clear the ways in which the use of technology begins to move from simple replacement to a transformation of the ways in which people engage with each other and the legal process.

Replacing People

Technology is also being used in ways that reduce the need for human input into the resolution of disputes. Commentators have suggested that big data, the Internet of Things, natural language processing, generative AI and a rapidly expanding robotics industry have the potential to transform the world of work in even more fundamental ways than those discussed above (Morrison & Harkens, 2019). The ability of machines to take on tasks traditionally performed by humans is a particular risk to those lawyers who perform routine, relatively rule-bound tasks on a regular basis such as routine wills, conveyancing or bulk contracts. Artificial intelligence[10] is particularly well suited to change the work of lawyers involved in discovery, legal searches, document generation, and the prediction of case outcomes (Nissan, 2017). The latter is particularly significant in a civil justice system characterised by the high level of out of court settlements. These uses of technology are being driven by both the private and public sectors. Electronic litigation support technologies for lawyers began to emerge in the US in the 1960s to lessen the burden of manual processing of documents. Driven by demands from business clients to reduce the costs of litigation, large commercial law firms are now using AI to analyse large amounts of machine readable documentation during the discovery process; help lawyers identify precedents in case law; and support judges with predictions on issues including sentence duration and recidivism scores in the criminal justice system.[11] Rather than just processing, capturing, distributing, reproducing and disseminating information, programmes now in use benefit from the employment of techniques such as predictive coding,[12] text mining and automatic text summarisation to perform 'smart' tasks which would normally be undertaken by humans (Nissan, 2017). This means that searching, retrieval, cross referencing, hyperlinks and annotation all became much easier, and the need to read documents repeatedly in preparation for negotiations or adjudication rendered unnecessary (Susskind, 2008). Indeed, the Chinese legal system now uses artificial intelligence to sift through private messages or comments on social media that can be used as evidence in court and has more than 100 robots in courts across the country which reduces the workload of officials by retrieving case histories and past verdicts. Some of the robots even have legal specialisms, such as commercial law or labour-related disputes (Harris, 2017).

The application of computational techniques to the analysis and synthesis of documents through natural language processing also promises further innovations in the way that documents are managed, analysed, and understood. Natural language processing aims to copy the human skills involved in interpreting complex information and to reduce decision-making to a large decision tree or a structured body of rules. In this way, human knowledge is unpacked and standardised by machines and in doing so undermines the claims of lawyers to possess rarefied knowledge. Moreover, in the new drive to commodify knowledge previously guarded by lawyers, computer engineers have an interest in exposing and commodifying the standardised and routine nature of as much legal work as possible (Susskind, 2008). Indeed, Goldman Sachs has estimated that generative AI is capable of automating 44% of legal tasks in the US including such things as drafting, document review, predicting case outcomes to inform strategy and engaging in settlement negotiations (Vos, 2023).

As with many developments in the field, there is a drive from the private sector to increase the efficiency of litigation, especially in large-scale commercial disputes (Nissan, 2017). Lawyers specialising in litigation have long been interested in the possibility of generating early predictions of the likely success of a case. This has provided financial incentives to develop technological systems based on decision trees and probabilities which can use fact patterns and precedent to predict case outcomes. One example of this is the development of LexMachina in the US, in patent litigation which uses data on case characteristics, the lawyers and judges involved and outputs which is compiled, and enhanced by a unique combination of machine learning and in-house legal experts which is updated every 24 hours.[13] In some jurisdictions, most notably China, similar uses are being made of technology to help judges organise trial information, enhance research capabilities, reviewing evidence and testimony and compare with similar previous cases (Wang, 2020).

At the same time as disempowering professionals, it has been claimed that the production of standardised data collection methods can help people manage their own case, create their own legal documents, and put law within the reach of the laity.[14] A further development in the capacity of machines to help humans negotiate settlements is exemplified by 'JusticeBot' a legal decision support tool developed in the cyberjustice lab in Montreal (Westermann et al., 2023). This software tool asks people a number of questions about their dispute and, using Artificial Intelligence (AI), draws on cases with similar characteristics to provide users with information about similar previous cases and outcomes. The idea is that by doing so it enables users to gain a better understanding of their situation and the risks involved in pursuing a case to hearing. The system currently focuses on conflicts between landlords and tenants, but it has been claimed that the methodology and tools will be useable in many legal domains in the future.[15] In England and Wales there are plans to provide users of the legal system with 'Early Legal Services and Advice', some of which will be provided by AI drawing on a limited database of quality-assured materials to ensure its accuracy (Vos, 2023). Elsewhere it has been claimed that judges in Colombia, Bolivia, India, China, and Pakistan have used ChatGPT for advice on an issue during the determination of a case (Kennedy, 2023).

Technological innovation is also altering what the legal system can do by shifting its focus from the resolution of individual disputes to a focus on preventing future disputes and instigating systemic change. Sifting through a huge mass of data on cases to come up with patterns about certain types of problems, the issues at stake, the people involved and outcomes, opens up possibilities to chart trends and systemic failures that were unimaginable in earlier centuries. In the private sector the online dispute resolution systems introduced by eBay are considered paradigmatic in this context. By studying patterns of disputes, eBay has managed to identify common sources of problems and to structure information and services on its site so that these problems do not recur.[16] Dispute resolution theorists might claim that this has always been a function of courts, which send out important messages to potential litigants who are then able to bargain in the shadow of the law (Mnookin & Korhauser, 1978). But what is being mooted here is different; it involves an aspiration to instigate systemic change in the systems that cause problems rather than just future litigant behaviour. In the words of Rabinovich-Einy and Katsh (2014):

> The growth in use of [online dispute resolution] can therefore be expected to shine more light on the variables that underlie the emergence of conflicts and lead to efforts to respond to causes of problems, thereby blurring conceptual, and not only physical boundaries. The separation of dispute prevention and dispute resolution, which seems natural in a world that did not stress the sharing of information, begins to feel unnatural in an environment that revolves around processing and communicating data. (p. 27)[17]

By way of example, in a UK setting the Traffic Penalty Tribunal routinely uses national data collected by their system to plot different patterns of decision-making across local authorities in ways that allow them to judge their approach to penalty charge notices with other authorities (Mulcahy, 2024).

The potential for AI to rid the legal system of the unconscious bias of humans, which inevitably creeps into decision-making is also being mooted. Machines have the benefit of not experiencing fatigue, boredom, and other frailties which impact the quality of decision-making and have a greater capacity to work on a large number of cases simultaneously. Despite these benefits, few academic commentators are confident about the ability of AI to reach appropriate decisions in every case put before them and research has also demonstrated that AI, systems can also perpetuate existing biases (Mayson, 2018). In the words of Sourdin (2018):

> The role of a judge is a complex one. It can incorporate activism, complex interactions with people, dispute settlement, case management, public and specific education activities, social commentary as well as adjudicatory functions that might be conducted with other judges or less commonly in some jurisdictions with lay people (juries). The extent to which judges are engaged in each activity varies across jurisdictions and between judges. Some judges may be more 'responsive' than others, and others may show more emotion and compassion or be oriented towards therapeutic justice - interventions focussed on procedural justice that emphasise 'voice' and respect. Given this variation, it is difficult to determine how developments in artificial intelligence ('AI') may reshape the judicial role. (p. 1115)

It has been argued that there is a danger that system designers frequently assume that the making of legal judgements involves clear rules based on the logic of what is permissible or forbidden and straightforward fact patterns. While this is occasionally true and maybe a logical position to take in relation to the sort of low-level disputes which might arise when buying a product from eBay, it is far from being a universal position in the more complex disputes managed by the legal system on a daily basis. Most lawyers would see law as inherently ambiguous and as frequently requiring the exercise of discretion. For Morison and Harkens (2019) this simplistic approach to understanding what lawyers do is in danger of ignoring the subtle ways in which judges often resist certain applications of rules or open up new interpretations of them.

Despite these reservations, in March 2019, it was announced that Estonia had started to explore the use of an AI-based programme to decide small claims disputes (Ulenaers, 2020). Closer to home, Sir Geoffrey Vos has controversially suggested that as the legal is digitalised, AI might also be used to decide some 'less intensely personal disputes', such as commercial cases (Kennedy, 2023). In his words:

> As for robo-judging, the controls that will be required are (a) for the parties to know what decisions are taken by judges and what by machines, and (b) for there always to be the option of taking a case to appeal to allow it to be scrutinised by a human judge. The limiting feature for machine-made decisions is likely to be the requirement that the users have confidence in that system. There are some decisions – like for example intensely personal ones relating to the welfare of children – that humans are unlikely ever to accept being decided by machines. But in other kinds of disputes, such as commercial and compensation disputes, parties may come to have confidence in machine made decisions more quickly than many might expect. (Vos, 2023, para 19)

China launched the world's first 'smart court' in 2017 which is presided over by AI powered judges. Early evaluations of the development have identified concerns about the bias produced by the 'black box' or opaqueness of AI algorithms which threaten to undermine the legitimacy of the process. It has been argued that when faced with complex cases involving ethical issues and legal values the decisions reached are in danger of being inconclusive or inappropriate, but could be improved by multi-disciplinary design involving those other than engineers (Wang, 2020). Fears that the higher order cognitive functions will not be adequately performed by machines however well-programmed are particularly significant to scholars interested in procedural justice where the focus is, amongst other things on the importance of citizens feeling heard and assured that they are treated with respect. This issue goes straight to the heart of the debate about the extent to which the legal system should be seen as a service that is outcome orientated or an institution that is driven by civic values. This is a question to which we return in the next chapter.

Conclusion

This chapter has discussed how technology is capable of changing the ways in which documents are filed, analysed, organised and accessed and how people and machines interact with each other and the legal system. The systems described include those that are technologically simple, those that are highly advanced or only just being imagined. The systems discussed towards the end of this chapter are only being conceived of, built, developed, and evaluated by computer engineers. At the same time, issues of equity arise in relation to who has access to these new technological resources. Many of the sophisticated systems in constant use in large commercial law firms can only be imagined by poorly funded lawyers who work in the legal aid and not-for-profit sector.

Whatever is imagined as possible by engineers, neither digitisation nor the forms of digital transformation discussed in this chapter can occur without a sophisticated technological infrastructure in place. Even the success of something as simple as e-filing relies on there being large scale and secure storage available for legal systems that deal with thousands of cases each year involving millions of pieces of confidential information from multiple sources. The reality is that the majority of legal systems are nowhere close to realising the forms of digital transformation discussed by techno-evangelicals, even if they choose to do so. As was argued in the last chapter, the English and Welsh legal system is still struggling to get some courts and judges equipped with adequate computers or secured shared drives.

Far from rendering discussion about the possibilities of technology in a legal setting redundant, considerations of what is possible and now being imagined provide us with important opportunities to engage with the rhetoric that frequently fuels reform before systems are transformed further. One key issue that arises is whether what is suitable in the private domain should act as an example for the public sector. This is important as companies such as eBay are treated as exemplars that are leading the way in managing high volumes of low-level disputes in ways that may or may not be appropriate in the public sector.

The more one studies digital technologies in the legal system, the more difficult it becomes to present a neutral chronology or account of technological developments. When viewed from the perspective of the policymaker or engineer, the approach adopted is frequently solution driven, focusing on the functionality or internal logic of the system created rather than the power dynamics that lie behind it. While sympathy for user driven design is far from absent in the examples we cite, there is considerable scope for more attention to be paid to the needs of the citizen rather than just the system. In his blistering account of the UK's approach to the development of technological solutions and the collision between technology and democracy, Fishenden (2023) has argued that insufficient attention has been paid to joining up government systems with a view to single entry portals for a range of services. Without sensitivity to the need for responsible innovation, there is a danger that technology is inappropriately treated as synonymous with progress, or framed as the choice between modernisation or mummification. These are issues which we go on to discuss in the next chapters.

Notes

1. https://e-justice.europa.eu/home?action=home
2. https://www.disabilityrightsuk.org/news/2019/september/new-hmcts-webchat-service-give-social-security-appeal-guidance-and-support
3. Legally represented parties **must** use the Electronic Working Scheme to issue proceedings and applications in the Commercial Court but litigants in person do not have to. See further: https://www.judiciary.uk/courts-and-tribunals/business-and-property-courts/commercial-court/litigating-in-the-commercial-court/fees-filing-and-forms/e-filing-electronic-working-scheme/; and https://www.justice.gov.uk/courts/procedure-rules/civil/rules/part51/practice-direction-51o-the-electronic-working-pilot-scheme
4. As of June 2023 it was possible in England and Wales to securely submit, pay for and manage cases online in a number of hearing centres including the *Business and Property Courts, Court of Appeal (Civil Division), Employment Appeal Tribunal, High Court Family Appeals, King's Bench Division*, claims and appeals in some of the Royal Courts of Justice, the *Senior Courts Costs Office* and four of the upper. See further: https://www.gov.uk/guidance/the-hmcts-reform-programme#what-weve-achieved

5. A holographic display is a 3D display that presents a three-dimensional image to the viewer without the need for them to wear any special glasses or use other equipment.
6. The hologram witnesses appeared as though they are in the courtroom, albeit behind a piece of glass and with a several second delay when responding to questions.
7. https://www.expertservices.com/insight/courtroom-technology-on-the-horizon/
8. https://rechtwijzer.nl/rechtwijzer/; https://jaarverslag.raadvoorrechtsbijstand.org/rechtwijzer-voorziet-behoefte/
9. https://libraryguides.missouri.edu/c.php?g=557240&p=3832248
10. Artificial intelligence refers to the intelligence of machines or computer systems, and is an incredibly rapidly developing field, so it is entirely possible, if not likely, that the information in this book would have developed further from the time of writing. AI enables technology to complete a whole range of tasks from searching, analysing, and compiling information, drafting contracts, assigning resources, such as judicial time, and even the possibility of algorithms deciding on the outcome of a case. It is a very diverse field, with an enormous range of variable applications in the legal sector.
11. https://www.unesco.org/en/artificial-intelligence/rule-law/mooc-judges
12. Predictive data mining whose aim is to learn from sample data in order to make a prediction and whose techniques include neural networks, rule induction, linear, multiple regression.
13. https://lexmachina.com/
14. Susskind (2008) cites the US LegalZoom company as an example of a company that enables people to create legal documents such as wills, incorporate businesses, register trademarks with lawyers available online to support decisions. See further: https://www.legalzoom.com/country/gb
15. https://www.cyberjustice.ca/en/logiciels-cyberjustice/nos-solutions-logicielles/justicebot
16. The are some precedents for this in the English civil justice system, most notably the setting up of the Faculty of Learning by NHS Resolution which defends clinical negligence claims on behalf of the NHS. The Faculty takes the form of a repository of educational learning products and resources developed by NHS Resolution to support the health service to learn from errors made evident in the course of litigation. See: https://resolution.nhs.uk/faculty-of-learning/
17. For other examples of online dispute resolution systems see: Justice42 in the Netherlands; eBRAM in Hong Kong; Case Law Analytics in France; Matterhorn in the US.

Bibliography

Briggs, L. J. (2016). *Civil Courts Structure Review: Final Report by Lord Justice Briggs*. https://www.judiciary.uk/wp-content/uploads/2016/07/civil-courts-structure-review-final-report-jul-16-final-1.pdf

Fishenden, J. (2023). *Fracture: The Collision Between Technology and Democracy and How We Fix It*. Amazon.

Gander, L. (2002). *Applications of the Internet for Public Legal Education*. https://www.advicenow.org.uk/sites/default/files/uploads/2013/05/applications-of-the-internet-for-public-legal-education-gander-l-43.pdf

Harris, B. (2017). *Could an AI Ever Replace a Judge in Court?*, World Governments Summit. https://www.worldgovernmentsummit.org/observer/articles/2017/detail/could-an-ai-ever-replace-a-judge-in-court

Kennedy, R. (2023, 10 July). AI: Why Installing Robot Judges in Courtrooms is a Really Bad Idea *The Conversation*. https://theconversation.com/ai-why-installing-robot-judges-in-courtrooms-is-a-really-bad-idea-208718

Koshykar, M. B. (2004). E-Filing Court Documents: The Possibilities and Progress of E-Filing in New York State. *Syracuse Science & Technology: Law Reporter, 1*.

Krause, J. (2006). The Force of e-Filing. *ABAJ, 92*, 54.

Latour, B. (2010). *The Making of Law: An Ethnography of the Conseil d'Etat*. Polity.

Mayson, S. G. (2018). Bias in, Bias out. *Yale Law Journal, 128*(8), 2218–2301.

Menashe, D. (2017). A Critical Analysis of the Online Court. *University of Pennsylvania Journal, 39*, 921.

Mnookin, R. H., & Kornhauser, L. (1978). Bargaining in the Shadow of the Law: The Case of Divorce. *The Yale Law Journal, 88*, 950.

Morison, J., & Harkens, A. (2019). Re-engineering Justice? Robot Judges, Computerised Courts and (Semi) Automated Legal Decision-Making. *Legal Studies, 39*(4), 618–635.

Mulcahy, L. (2024). Modernisation or Transformation? User Led Design and the Facilitation of Systemic Change in the Traffic Penalty Tribunal. *Civil Justice Quarterly, 43*(2), 120–141.

National Audit Office. (2019). *The Challenges in Implementing Digital Change*, HC 575.

Nissan, E. (2017). Digital Technologies and Artificial Intelligence's Present and Foreseeable Impact on Lawyering, Judging, Policing and Law Enforcement. *AI & Society, 32*, 441–464.

Olugasa, O., & Davies, A. (2022). Remote Court Proceedings in Nigeria: Justice Online or Justice on the Line. *International Journal for Court Administration, 13*(2), 1

Rabinovich-Einy, O., & Katsh, E. (2014). Digital Justice: Reshaping Boundaries in an Online Dispute Resolution Environment. *International Journal of Online Dispute Resolution, 1*(1), 5–36.

Sloan, K. (2023, May 16). *Beam Me Up, Counselor. Are Hologram Witnesses Headed to Court?* https://www.reuters.com/legal/government/beam-me-up-counselor-are-hologram-witnesses-headed-court-2023-05-16/

Sourdin, T. (2018). Judge v Robot?: Artificial Intelligence and Judicial Decision-Making. *University of New South Wales Law Journal, 41*(4), 1114–1133.

Susskind, R. (2008). *The End of Lawyers*. Oxford University Press.

Tait, D., McKimmie, B. M., Sarre, R., Jones, D., McDonald, L. W., & Gelb, K. (2017). *Towards a Distributed Courtroom*. Retrieved from https://courtofthefuture.org/publications/towards-distributed-courtroom/

Ulenaers, J. (2020). The Impact of Artificial Intelligence on the Right to a Fair Trial: Towards a Robot Judge? *Asian Journal of Law and Economics, 11*(2).

Westermann, H., Meeùs, S., Godet, M., Troussel, A., Tan, J., Savelka, J., & Benyekhlef, K. (2023). *Bridging the Gap: Mapping Layperson Narratives to Legal Issues with Language Models*. Proceedings of the Sixth Workshop on Automated Semantic Analysis of Information in Legal Text (ASAIL 2023).

Vos, G. (2023, June 21, Thursday). *Speech by the Master of the Rolls to the Bar Council of England and Wales*, 20th Annual Law Reform Lecture, Lincolns Inn. https://www.judiciary.uk/speech-by-the-master-of-the-rolls-to-the-bar-council-of-england-and-wales/

Wang, N. (2020, November). "Black Box Justice": Robot Judges and AI-based Judgment Processes in China's Court System. In *2020 IEEE International Symposium on Technology and Society (ISTAS)* (pp. 58–65). IEEE.

CHAPTER 3

What Is Gained When Justice Moves Online?

Abstract This chapter explores the many benefits of online justice. It argues that moving justice online not only offers the chance to make legal systems more efficient and accessible but also provides the opportunity to reimagine how we facilitate greater engagement between citizens and the state. The chapter illustrates the urgent need to move away from romanticised accounts of the courtroom as a pseudo-sacred space, which socio-legal accounts of courtroom dynamics and legal process have frequently found to be false. While remaining sceptical about the claims of techno-evangelicals, it examines how new technologies can remake the spatial and temporal world of the justice system with a view to greater accessibility and sensitivity to the needs of the disadvantaged.

Keywords Technological advantages · Online justice · Accessibility · Video hearings

INTRODUCTION

The technological changes being introduced to legal systems across the world offer a plethora of advantages to the citizen. These innovations mean that users of the justice system can access online information about their rights and how to assert them which would previously have involved a trip to a library, advice centre, or lawyer. Disputants can now initiate and engage in legal processes at a distance when they were previously required to travel to a justice centre or courthouse at some distance from their home. They can now do things quickly online at a time that is convenient to them which would previously have involved the production, copying and physical delivery of documents. In short, digitisation offers powerful tools for communicating, storing and processing information which can make asserting and enforcing rights easier than it has ever been. As Abdel-Wahab et al. (2012) have argued, the computer has moved dispute resolution into the home, the workplace or any other place which is convenient for the citizen.

In addition to rendering justice systems faster and more flexible, technology is also responding to changes in the ways people interact in contemporary societies and the new types of disputes which computerisation has made now possible. This is most evident in the field of online commerce in which online dispute resolution has become the norm; an industry as well as a process (Katsh & Rifkin, 2001). For some, paper-based institutions appear increasingly outmoded in a society in which a significant proportion of everyday activity can be conducted using the internet (Katsh & Rabinovich-Einy, 2017). These changing attitudes can be expected to impact the public as well as the private sector and bring transformations in what people expect from the State justice system. As discussed in Chapter 2, in time this might include an expectation that software programmes using data collected from the justice system will prevent disputes in the future as well as resolving them in the present. Thinking about technology in these ways encourages us to reimagine the justice system as a public service for citizens rather than just a place (Susskind, 2021), to reflect on its key aims, to determine who we want it to serve, and to develop innovative ways in which to better deliver these ends.

This chapter explores what the justice system and its users gain by going online. While remaining sceptical about the ambitious claims of techno-evangelicals, it will consider how new technologies can remake the spatial and temporal world of the legal system and enhance meaningful engagement with the justice system for lay and disadvantaged participants. The first section explores the limitations of a justice system that relies on bricks, mortar, rarefied spaces, and physical presence. In doing so, it argues that it is essential to examine the systems and places that technological developments are designed to replace; not least because there is a danger that technological naysayers frequently romanticise the courthouse as a pseudo-sacred spaces which socio-legal accounts of courtroom dynamics have frequently found to be false. The second section considers how online hearings can provide solutions to these concerns and create a more immediate, connected, and democratic legal space. The third section will explore the many advantages offered by the move online including greater efficiency, accessibility, transparency and openness. The last section will take a more radical view of what future changes may lie ahead, and how technology provides us with the tools to rethink and reimagine the court service.

Journeys into the Legal System

Access to justice is frequently judged in terms of the number of people who use the legal system.[1] The reason for this focus is clear. Generations of socio-legal scholars have revealed the problems people face in knowing what constitutes a justiciable problem, accessing legal services, or knowing how to present their case (Denvir et al., 2012, 2014; Pleasence et al., 2017). It is clear that early expert advice can prevent untenable claims being pursued at considerable expense to the citizen and that technology has much to offer the field (Knake, 2013). As Law for Life (2023) has claimed:

> The intersection of public legal education and technology has the potential to democratise access to justice, empowering individuals to better understand their legal rights and access the resources they need to resolve legal issues. As technology continues to evolve, so too will the opportunities to leverage it in the service of public legal education.

Though the information currently available for the public is not uniformly of a high quality, the internet appears to be playing a growing role in the resolution strategies of many of those who face civil justice problems (Denvir, 2016). By way of example, the Citizens Advice website provides easily comprehensible guidance on finding free or affordable legal help [2]; reporting rape and sexual assault; going to court without a solicitor or barrister; acting as a witness in a legal hearing and making a small claim.[3] Once this advice was only available in person or by phone, but can now be provided by on websites, email, by webchat or by using a phone line. These systems are being well used, with the Citizens Advice impact report for 2022–2023 indicating that they had some 42.7 million visits to their website within the previous twelve months (Citizens Advice, 2023). Online information services are particularly valuable in areas where there is an uneven dispersal of advice services. It has been calculated that in the UK 12.45 million people live in housing advice deserts, often in rural locations, with another 1.09 million for family advice and 2.12 million for crime (LexisNexis, 2022).

Online public information, when well drafted and sensitive to the needs of a range of users, can educate the public from the comfort of their home, be read as many times as is desired and at a pace that works for those accessing it (Tsalapatanis & Mulcahy, 2023). Other key advantages are that information can be updated quickly and links to other networks of specialist information made available using hyperlinks. There is also the possibility of providing links to videos, podcasts, and other media to convey information. For instance, the Courts and Tribunals Service has made effective use of short videos to help people understand what happens at legal hearings and how to prepare for them.[4] In other instances, public sector organisations such as the Parliamentary and Health Service Ombudsman have made available a simple online decision tree or complaint checker to help people determine whether they have the jurisdiction to investigate a complaint about the health service.[5]

The JusticeBot developed by the Cyberjustice lab in Montreal, mentioned in the last chapter, is an example of the next generation of legal advice available online. Accessible from a computer, tablet, or smart phone, this software tool uses Artificial Intelligence (AI) to simplify access to legal information for the public involved in disputes between landlords and tenants. The tool guides the user through a series of questions about their case and then provides information about the outcomes of similar cases which enable users to assess the strength of their case and how to frame their claim. Between its launch in 2021 and 2023 JusticeBot has been used over 20,000 times in total with 65% of users being tenants (Westermann & Benyekhlef, 2023). Whether the system is commensurate with, or superior to, expert advice delivered face to face has yet to be seen but it certainly seems to be satisfying some unmet demand.

Online platforms now have the capacity to help litigants in person frame their dispute in ways that help to bring out key facts, issues and evidence. Technology can make the online initiation and pursuit of a legal claim far more user-friendly than traditional paper-based versions by using drop down menus for responses to common questions, automatically identifying parts of the form that have not been completed and customising questions in line with earlier responses (Hagan, 2022, 2023). These systems also have the capacity to provide pop up boxes with key definitions, links to pieces of legislation, or can promote greater speed and efficiency by providing autofill functions or copying information from other sources. Document automation of this kind can also provide considerable efficiency gains for judges (Susskind, 2023, p. 148).[6]

The new Divorce Online system launched in England and Wales in 2018 is an excellent example of a user-based approach to design that seeks to minimise mistakes and guide the applicant through the system in a way that makes sense to them. Using an online form in which the language previously used on paper forms has been simplified, it provides a computerised tour through the information needed by the state in order to process a divorce application. Users of the system are asked a series of progressively customised questions and are not allowed to proceed to the next screen until they have answered the questions on the current one. If the applicant does not have key information such as their marriage certificate, the system provides a link to another government website where a copy of the document can be ordered. A 'contact for help' link also appears on every page and gives access to out-of-hours webchat, an online messaging service, or an office hours telephone advice line. Documents can also be uploaded onto the site and the registry fee paid online. The Ministry of Justice reported soon after the national launch of the system that there had been a 95% drop in the number of applications being returned because of mistakes made by lay users (Bowcott, 2018). There are numerous other examples of the way in which software programmes support people in articulating their cases. Youstice, an online dispute resolution channel for commercial disputes offers parties the option to describe their position by selecting from a series of phrases and the site also suggests suitable solutions which can help in the course of negotiations.[7] Elsewhere, the Canadian Civil Resolution Tribunal, 'Solution Explorer' has self-help tools, such as communication templates.[8]

In addition to the benefits to consumers, these digital case management systems, when implemented correctly, have the scope to improve the efficiency of the legal system and reduce costs to the taxpayer. Large files may be manipulated more efficiently digitally, documents can be searched more easily, corrected instantly, and organised through a range of labelling and classifications systems (Rabinovich-Einy, 2008). Beyond their ability to centrally collect, distribute and manage case information, these systems also provide the opportunity to better allocate resources such as judicial workload and hearing space and can act as a diagnostic tool that gives courts a better understanding of their workflow (Wallace, 2013, p. 20).

Experiences of Trials and Hearings

Many of the spatial configurations of physical courtrooms now in use can be traced back centuries and tradition such as wood panelling and a prominent coat of arms are often said to add to the dignity and gravity of legal hearings. There is no doubt that the scale, layout, beauty and grandeur of some courts can inspire awe, and in his discussion of historic courthouses Binney (SAVE, 2004) has argued that:

> The special quality of historic courthouses lies in grand classical (and occasionally gothic) architecture, but above all in well fitted out interiors. The best are as perfectly fitted out examples of the joiner's art as an eighteenth century box-pewed church. Yet while the nineteenth century ecclesiologists stripped out or cut down almost every box pew, the conservatism of the legal profession ensured that many courtrooms survived unaltered from previous centuries. There are columned and domed interiors to compare to the finest city churches, interiors with seating as complete as in the finest surviving Georgian theatres. (p. 2)

A review of the court estate in the first decades of the twenty-first century presents us with a very different picture. Many historic courts are no longer fit for purpose and the majority of those built since the 1970s are mundane or have a corporate rather than a civic aesthetic. Recent government reports have documented how '[e]xisting court buildings are dilapidated and sometimes lack the basics, such as facilities for disabled users' (House of Commons Justice Committee, 2019, p. 3). In a similar vein, Lord Burnett, former Lord Chief Justice of England and Wales, has described much of the court estate as 'dilapidated and uncomfortable' and 'frankly, an embarrassment' (2018, p. 3). It has also been argued that the number and nature of available spaces do not meet the scale of existing needs and frequently cause a hearings backlog (House of Commons Committee of Public Accounts, 2022). Some of these problems could be remedied by re-opening courts or building new facilities but the decade between 2010 and 2020, saw the closure of 51% of Magistrates Courts (Sturge, 2020), and a third of County Courts (Cowie & Sturge, 2019) in England and Wales.

Research on approaches to the design of courthouses, and litigants' experiences of using them, suggests that problems with the design of the physical estate are more entrenched and frequently marginalise the needs of the public. It has been argued that the design of court buildings has been fundamental to the exercise of power by the privileged and has regularly prioritised the needs of professional users. In their account of the debate about the design of courts, from the 1970s to the present day, Mulcahy and Rowden (2019) discovered that the cross-departmental working group of civil servants responsible for producing a series of court design guides for England and Wales *never* consulted the public about their needs, despite regular an in-depth consultation with judges, barristers and solicitors. They argue that this has resulted in the interior design of courthouses becoming increasingly un-democratic, as a renewed focus has been placed on the segregation of participants and increasing attention has been paid to the claim that the laity is a security risk (see also Rock, 1993). Particular concerns have been raised about the presence of the dock in criminal courtrooms which separates defendants from their lawyers and places them at the margins of the court. Research has shown how docks, especially the increasingly popular secure docks,[9] can hamper the defendant's effective participation in a trial (JUSTICE, 2015; Mulcahy, 2013; Mulcahy et al., 2020a) or impact the presumption of innocence (Rossner et al., 2017). Another example of the tendency to marginalise the public in civil and criminal courts is the public gallery which is positioned in modern courts in ways that deliberately interrupt sightlines within the courtroom, for fear that the laity will intimidate others (Mulcahy & Rowden, 2019). While it is clearly possible to redesign courthouses to make them more inclusive and non-hierarchical (Tait, 2018), this would involve a considerable shift in attitudes.

Generations of criminological and socio-legal scholars have alluded to the ways in which the design of physical courts serves to alienate those who use them (Graham, 2003; Mulcahy & Rowden, 2019). Pat Carlen's (1976) early work on the Magistrates Court, most brutally articulated the ways in which the organisation of space in the modern courtroom can have a paralysing effect on lay users and contribute to what she describes as routine degradation rituals and sterile theatricality (Carlen, 1976). Over a decade later, Paul Rock's (1993) study of Wood Green Crown Court, drew attention to hierarchies of space within the courthouse. Other studies have explored the ways in which the spatial configuration of a courthouse can exacerbate the anxiety experienced by lay users by rendering them out of place or positioning them in close proximity to their adversary (Shapland et al., 1985). Most recently, attention has been drawn to the ways in which jurors, victims, witnesses, defendants, supporters and spectators experience the courtroom as outsiders, with rituals they find baffling solemnised through the design of space, arcane language, and dress. The courtroom experience for these participants is commonly perceived as something remote, foreign and elite rather than accessible, legible, and equitable (Jacobson et al., 2015). These findings begin to hint at the ways in which the internal configurations of the physical courthouse can impact the ability of citizens to effectively participate in the justice system. The key question for the purposes of this chapter is whether online proceedings can mitigate these problems.

For some commentators, moving online provides fresh opportunities to put lay users and their needs at the centre of design (Mulcahy & Rowden, 2019), and to think about the creation of new rituals which do not rely on outmoded concepts of hierarchy and justice (Rossner, 2021; Rossner & Tait, 2023; Rossner et al., 2017). A burgeoning body of research suggests that online hearings in which people appear alongside each other in standardised boxes had the capacity to render everyone in the trial equally important and improve the visibility of what happens in hearings. Rather than being required to sit behind their lawyer, clients appear alongside them online and can use messaging services to discreetly contact them. Those in the public gallery can enjoy uninterrupted sightlines.

The awe-inspiring architecture of physical courts can also be replaced by spaces that participants chose to appear from; which are familiar and comfortable. During an online jury trial experiment, run by the British NGO JUSTICE during the COVID pandemic lockdown, it was argued by those who took part that online hearings resulted in an improved sense of participation, a more level playing field and minimised the stress of attending a court building (Mulcahy et al., 2020b, p. 4). Elsewhere, in the Special Educational Needs and Disability Tribunal there is early evidence that children or adults whose needs are being considered are much more likely to join a hearing if it is online. Virtual hearings are particularly attractive to those individuals with neurodiverse conditions which render visiting new or unfamiliar spaces particularly stressful (Mulcahy et al., 2022).

In the criminal justice sphere, one of the most compelling cases for the use of online facilities relates to vulnerable adults and children who fear being in close proximity to those they have accused. These categories include survivors of rape, sexual or domestic abuse and coercive control. Experiments have also suggested that online hearings are less prejudicial for defendants in criminal trials who might otherwise appear from a segregated and enclosed dock (Rossner & Tait, 2023). Prisoners on remand may also prefer to attend a preliminary hearing online in order to avoid an uncomfortable trip in a prison van, missing meals or the risk of being moved to another prison after the trial (Transform Justice as cited in Select Committee on the Constitution, 2021, para. 84). In addition, there is emerging evidence that online proceedings that occur without everyone being visible can eliminate disparities and biases associated with visible identity markers such as race (Mentovich et al., 2019).[10]

Online trials can promote effective participation in the hearings. Disability groups have, for instance, drawn attention to the ways in which the move to online hearings has 'overwhelmingly benefited' disabled clients who were no longer required to travel great distances to attend hearings (as cited in Select Committee on the Constitution, 2021, para. 84). The Equal Treatment Bench Book (Courts & Tribunals Judiciary, 2023) has identified online hearings as a 'desirable adjustment' for certain participants including those with disabilities. Other examples of categories of people who would find online participation more convenient include those with caring responsibilities, those on low incomes now expected to travel greater distances to a courthouse following court closures, those who live in remote rural communities (Bailey et al., 2013), time-poor expert witnesses from other jurisdictions and geographically remote courtroom interpreters (Grieshofer, 2023). Speaking on the issue of online hearings Lord Burnett of Maldon, the former Lord Chief Justice of England and Wales has argued:

> If parties and witnesses are able to appear via their computers, it will be easier for them to fit their court appearances around their lives. Hitherto, we have required lives to be fitted around court appearances (however short) with the attendant travelling, wasting time, inconvenience, and interruption of work or domestic activities. (2018)

The logic here, of fitting hearings around lives, provides a significant departure from previous thinking about the importance of gathering and physical proximity to others in a collective enterprise.

Another way in which accessibility can be achieved is through continuous or asynchronous hearings which keep the justice system open 24/7. Sir Ernest Ryder has outlined what this model might look like in the context of social welfare tribunals:

> All participants, the appellant, the respondent [...] and the tribunal judge, are able to iterate and comment upon the basic case papers online, over a reasonable window of time, so that the issues in dispute can be clarified and explored. There is no need for all the parties to be together in a court or building at the same time. There is no single trial or hearing in the traditional sense. Our new approach is similar to that already used in other jurisdictions, where the trial process is an iterative one that stretches over a number of stages that are linked together. In our model, however, we will not need those stages to take place in separate hearings or indeed, unless it is necessary, any physical, face to face hearing at all. We will have a single, digital hearing that is continuous over an extended period of time. (2016)

The idea of the continuous hearing disrupts traditional unities of time, space and action in trials, but in doing so gives time for valuable pauses in interactions and minimises the emotional intensity of a more tightly choreographed time bound event. In the UK, the work of the Traffic Penalty Tribunal (TPT) is frequently referred to as being at the forefront of such innovations (see for instance Adler [2016] and Thomas and Tomlinson [2017]). Appellants can register their case, explain what happened in their own words and upload evidence to their online case file at a time convenient to them. This includes annotated photographs, drawings, screenshots of messages, short films and documents that can be produced by a smartphone. The Resolver platform, designed to assist UK consumers in resolving complaints against companies, allows users to create a personal case file for each issue, manage the case file by themselves by adding evidence, replying to communications from the other parties, tracking the progress or downloading materials on to their own devices. These developments have been described as a new form of 'process pluralism', in which a range of procedural choices or mediums are offered in order to make hearings better adapted to the needs of the particular parties and issues at hand (Rabinovich-Einy, 2022).

Rendering Justice More Open

Open justice is at the heart of Western and democratic concepts of what renders a legal system legitimate. At a practical level, it involves allowing members of the public to attend and observe hearings or gain access to documents relating to them; permitting journalists to report on proceedings and generally ensuring that hearings are open to public scrutiny. Open justice has also been seen as having an educational function, informing the public of how the legal system works (Jaconelli, 2002). Despite the importance of these aspirations, it could be argued that open justice has been declining in recent years as a result of the reduction in the number of members of the public attending trials (Graham, 2003), and the decline of local journalism and funding cuts in the media more broadly. Bosland and Townend (2018) have concluded that as a result of these changes: 'the media no longer have the resources or sufficient inclination to adequately safeguard the public interest in transparency in the courts' (p. 1).

Live streaming of trials or granting access to those who request to join an online public gallery, is a clear solution to these problems. It also facilitates people not having to travel long distances to observe trials and avoids the degradation of having to go through security checkpoints. During the COVID-19 pandemic, a pressing open justice concern was how to allow the public into online hearings, and it has been suggested that the issue was not well handled (Townend & Magrath, 2021). Despite this, there are several examples of livestreaming of trials and hearings working well which could provide useful models for the future. These include the system put in place by the UK Supreme Court and the International Criminal Court.[11]

Being able to view hearings and the documents associated with them remotely also makes it easier for journalists to cover what is happening in the courts. Speaking of these issues and some of the changes that were implemented in Australia during the pandemic, Karen Percy from the Australian Broadcasting Corporation explains:

> There is increased pressure on journalists, [...], which is going to make it harder to keep up our scrutiny of the court system. Ideally, you do things in real time in court, but easier online access to documents and court files – like in the County Court [of Victoria, Australia] – and the ability to watch web-streams, will become more important to ensuring the media can properly cover the courts. (as cited in Robinson & Lewis, 2020)

As this quotation indicates, online facilitated open justice requires more than a livestreaming of trials or sending out links to those who request them. It also requires much more efficient dissemination of information online about what trials and hearings are taking place. The House of Commons Justice Committee has explained:

> Court and tribunal lists were traditionally only pinned to notice boards inside court buildings. This may have worked well in a pre-digital age, when there was a greater number of dedicated court reporters who spent much of their time effectively stationed inside our court and tribunal buildings, but the public and media now expect to be able to access such information instantaneously on their phones and laptops. (House of Commons Justice Committee, 2023, p. 4)

These changes are already underway in England and Wales, with the 'Court and Tribunal Hearing Service' providing listings online at a range of courthouses, with plans to expand to others (HM Courts & Tribunal Service, 2023). In time, public users could be more openly encouraged to view hearings in advance as preparation for their own case, or to better understand what form the process will take. This could all be done using a simple hyperlink from the court or tribunal's webpage.

It has also been suggested that the shift to digital can make other parts of the justice system more transparent. The digital systems now being realised, whether they involve case management, digital listing, or fully online hearings, are capable of capturing significant amounts of data and metadata.[12] These can be analysed in order to monitor and scrutinise the justice system. In their 2016 report, the Lord Chancellor, the Lord Chief Justice, and the Senior President of Tribunals (2016) highlighted how the collection and greater availability of data regarding the justice system will help with accountability and transparency. Academics have long bemoaned the lack of such data and have an important role to play in using the data that digital transformation is creating in order to help plot trends and developments in the justice system. This may mean making de-identified data easily accessible and providing funding to create capacity for analysis, but the potential for greater scrutiny of the justice system from outside of it is significant.

Conclusion

This chapter has charted a number of the most significant ways in which technology can improve how people access the legal system, their experiences once they are in it and the ways in which the general public and academic community can ensure that there is adequate scrutiny of the justice system. Each of these factors draws on fundamental concepts that underpin the justice systems of advanced democracy, not least of which are the rule of law, fair trials and open justice. In an era in which there is considerable debate about the democratic deficit and ways in which the populace is losing their faith in the ability of elites to run public services in a way that benefits the disadvantaged, these issues are of considerable significance. Indeed, it could be argued that the very legitimacy of the legal system depends on greater accessibility, transparency and accountability. It is clear from research that the justice system is not as accessible as it needs to be, that there is unmet legal need and that many are forced to abandon their legal claims or defences because of a lack of knowledge, support, or resources. Responsible and user-led design of new technologies makes it possible to remedy a number of these problems and to rethink the purpose of legal process and adjudication.

Notes

1. This can be defined as providing people with awareness, knowledge and understanding of rights and legal issues together with the confidence and skills they need to deal with disputes and gain access to justice (Wintersteiger et al., 2021).
2. The Public Law Project and Transform Justice suggest that in certain circumstances legal advice costs can be reduced when consultation with clients are conducted online (Select Committee on the Constitution, 2021, para. 103). Furthermore, accessing advice digitally may in part help people living in remote areas or legal aid deserts to access advice.
3. See further: https://www.citizensadvice.org.uk/law-and-courts/.
4. https://www.youtube.com/playlist?list=PLORVvk_w75Py6JClMOiiltyTjI2gyc81g.
5. https://www.ombudsman.org.uk/#complaint-checker.
6. Unfortunately, despite these efficiencies, not all digital filing stays that way. An example of this is Money Claims Online, operating since 2001, which in 2016, despite having claims being lodged online, post lodging reverted paper-based system with 'a civil servant at the other end ha[ving] to print the e-form, and make up a paper file' (Ryder, 2016). Similarly, at the time of writing, 'significant proportions' of online probate and divorce cases 'required manual staff interventions although [HMCTS] classes the projects as complete' (National Audit Office, 2023, p. 9). Yet despite these discrepancies, these systems can prove to be more efficient. But digital does not always mean faster, and

there are international examples of where digital processes may actually take longer (Procopiuck, 2018).
7. https://www.judiciary.uk/wp-content/uploads/2015/02/Online-Dispute-Resolution-Final-Web-Version1.pdf. See also: https://www.odreurope.com/meet-justice.
8. See further: https://civilresolutionbc.ca/wp-content/uploads/CRT-Annual-Report-2022-2023.pdf. As an administrative tribunal, the CRT deals with certain types of civil disputes in British Columbia. The Civil Resolution Tribunal Act allows the CRT to handle small claims issues (up to $5000 related to things bought or sold, loans, personal property, contracts, roommates, pets, and others), vehicle accidents (entitlement to benefits, fault, damages, and/or minor injury determination), strata property (strata bylaws, councils, governance, maintenance and damage, nuisance, and others), societies and cooperative associations.
9. These are docks which are enclosed from the floor to the ceiling and effectively constitute a room within the courtroom.
10. In some jurisdictions experiments are being conducted using avatars which replicate the movements and facial expressions of live participants. One advantage of this development is said to be that participants could create a look which minimizes the chance of discrimination.
11. The Court of Appeal (Civil Division) has been streaming select cases from as early as 2019 via the Judiciary's YouTube channel. The website highlights that the purpose of this is 'to improve public access to, and understanding of, the work of the courts' and that they 'are working towards making it possible for all appropriate cases to be live streamed'. For more information see: https://www.judiciary.uk/the-court-of-appeal-civil-division-live-streaming-of-court-hearings/.
12. For those who don't know, metadata is data that provided information about other data, such as when it was added and who it was added by, and who may have made changes to it.

Bibliography

Abdel-Wahab, M. S. A., Katsh, E., & Rainey, D. (2012). Online Dispute Resolution for Africa. *Online Dispute Resolution: Theory and Practice a Treatise on Technology and Dispute Resolution*.

Adler, M. (2016). A New Leviathan: Benefit Sanctions in the Twenty-First Century. *Journal of Law and Society, 43*, 195.

Bailey, J., Burkell, J., & Reynolds, G. (2013). Access to Justice for All: Towards an Expansive Vision of Justice and Technology. *Windsor Yearbook of Access to Justice, 31*(2), 181–208.

Bosland, J. J., & Townend, J. (2018). Open Justice, Transparency and the Media: Representing the Public Interest in the Physical and Virtual Courtroom. *Communications Law, 23*(4), 183–202.

Bowcott, O. (2018, May 6). Log in, Break Up—New Easy Way to Get a Divorce Online. *The Observer.* https://www.theguardian.com/lifeandstyle/2018/may/06/easy-divorce-online-couples-avoid-stress-of-court

Carlen, P. (1976). The Staging of Magistrates' Justice. *The British Journal of Criminology, 16*(1), 48–55.

Citizens Advice. (2023). *Citizens Advice 2022–2023 Impact Report* [CA Impacy Report]. https://drive.google.com/file/d/1sXNi3WpeLOff8q6Bcl8yHvA8sf8DnamC/view

Courts and Tribunals Judiciary. (2023). *The Equal Treatment Bench Book (April 2023 Interim Revision).* https://www.judiciary.uk/wp-content/uploads/2023/06/Equal-Treatment-Bench-Book-April-2023-revision.pdf

Cowie, G., & Sturge, G. (2019). *Court Closures and Access to Justice* (House of Commons Debate Pack CDP-0156). https://researchbriefings.files.parliament.uk/documents/CDP-2019-0156/CDP-2019-0156.pdf

Denvir, C. (2016). Online and in the Know? Public Legal Education, Young People and the Internet. *Computers & Education, 92,* 204–220.

Denvir, C., Balmer, N. J., & Buck, A. (2012). Informed Citizens? Knowledge of Rights and the Resolution of Civil Justice Problems. *Journal of Social Policy, 41*(3), 591–614.

Denvir, C., Balmer, N. J., & Pleasence, P. (2014). Portal or Pot Hole? Exploring How Older People Use the 'Information Superhighway' for Advice Relating to Problems with a Legal Dimension. *Ageing & Society, 34*(4), 670–699.

Graham, C. (2003). *Ordering Law: The Architectural and Social History of the English Law Court to 1914.* Routledge.

Grieshofer, T. (2023). Remote Interpreting in Immigration Tribunals. *International Journal for the Semiotics of Law/Revue Internationale de Sémiotique Juridique, 36*(2), 767–788. https://doi.org/10.1007/s11196-022-09908-3

Hagan, M. (2022, June 30). How Do You Design a User-Friendly Court Form? Medium. https://medium.com/legal-design-and-innovation/how-do-you-design-a-user-friendly-court-form-ab241ed1e134

Hagan, M. (2023, March 2). Design Standards for Court & Government Forms. *Legal Design and Innovation.* https://medium.com/legal-design-and-innovation/design-standards-for-court-government-forms-c5e157e42b2

HM Courts and Tribunal Service. (2023, May). *Fact Sheet: Court and Tribunal Hearings Service.* GOV.UK. https://www.gov.uk/government/publications/hmcts-reform-infrastructure-and-enabling-services-fact-sheets/fact-sheet-court-and-tribunal-hearings-service

House of Commons Committee of Public Accounts. (2022). *Reducing the Backlog in Criminal Courts* (HC 643). https://publications.parliament.uk/pa/cm5802/cmselect/cmpubacc/643/report.html

House of Commons Justice Committee. (2019). *Court and Tribunal Reforms* (HC 190, Second Report of Session 2019). House of Commons. https://publications.parliament.uk/pa/cm201919/cmselect/cmjust/190/190.pdf

House of Commons Justice Committee. (2023). *Open Justice: Court Reporting in the Digital Age: Government Response to the Committee's Fifth Report of Session 2022–23* (HC 1040, Seventh Special Report of Session 2022–23).

Jacobson, J., Hunter, G., & Kirby, A. (2015). *Inside Crown Court: Personal Experiences and Questions of Legitimacy.* Policy Press.

Jaconelli, J. (2002). *Open Justice: A Critique of the Public Trial*. Oxford University Press.
JUSTICE. (2015). *In the Dock: Reassessing the Use of the Dock in Criminal Trials*. https://files.justice.org.uk/wp-content/uploads/2015/07/06170833/JUSTICE-In-the-Dock.pdf
Katsh, E. & Rabinovich-Einy, O., (2017). *Digital Justice: Technology and the Internet of Disputes*. Oxford University Press. https://doi.org/10.1093/acprof:oso/9780190464585.001.0001
Katsh, E., & Rifkin, J. (2001). *Online Dispute Resolution: Resolving Conflicts in Cyberspace*. Jossey-Bass.
Knake, R. N. (2013). Democratizing Legal Education. 'Democratizing Legal Education'. *Connecticut Law Review*, 197. https://opencommons.uconn.edu/law_review/197
Law for Life. (2023, March 7). *Public Legal Education and Technology*. Advicenow. https://www.advicenow.org.uk/lawforlife/public-legal-education-and-technology
LexisNexis. (2022). *The LexisNexis Legal Aid Deserts Report*. https://www.lexisnexis.co.uk/insights/the-lexisnexis-legal-aid-deserts-report/
Lord Burnett & House of Commons Justice Committee. (2018). *The Lord Chief Justice's Report* (HC 1651). https://committees.parliament.uk/oralevidence/8634/pdf/
Lord Burnett of Maldon, Lord Chief Justice of England and Wales. (2018, June 2). *The Age of Reform: Sir Henry Brooke Annual Lecture*. https://www.judiciary.uk/wp-content/uploads/2018/06/speech-lcj-the-age-of-reform2.pdf
Lord Chancellor, the Lord Chief Justice and the Senior President of Tribunals. (2016). *Transforming Our Justice System*. https://assets.publishing.service.gov.uk/government/uploads/system/uploads/attachment_data/file/553261/joint-vision-statement.pdf
Mack, K., & Anleu, S. R. (2007). 'Getting Through the List': Judgecraft and Legitimacy in the Lower Courts. *Social & Legal Studies*, 16(3), 341–361.
Mack, K., & Anleu, S. R. (2010). Performing Impartiality: Judicial Demeanor and Legitimacy. *Law & Social Inquiry*, 35(1), 137–173.
Mentovich, A., Prescott, J. J., & Rabinovich-Einy, O. (2019). Are Litigation Outcome Disparities Inevitable? Courts, Technology, and the Future of Impartiality. *Alabama Law Review*, 71(4), 893–980.
Mulcahy, L. (2013). Putting the Defendant in Their Place: Why Do We Still Use the Dock in Criminal Proceedings? *The British Journal of Criminology*, 53(6), 1139–1156. https://doi.org/10.1093/bjc/azt037
Mulcahy, L., Rossner, M., & Rowden, E. (2020a). *What If the Dock Was Abolished in Criminal Courts?* [What if?... Series of Challenging Pamphelts]. Howard League for Penal Reform. https://howardleague.org/wp-content/uploads/2020/01/What-if...-the-dock-was-abolished-1.pdf
Mulcahy, L., & Rowden, E. (2019). *The Democratic Courthouse: A Modern History of Design*. Routledge.
Mulcahy, L., Rowden, E., & Teeder, W. (2020b). *Testing the Case for a Virtual Courtroom with a Physical Jury Hub: Second Evaluation of a Virtual Trial Pilot Study Conducted by JUSTICE* [JUSTICE]. https://files.justice.org.uk/wp-content/uploads/2020/06/06165935/Mulcahy-Rowden-second-evaluation-report-JUSTICE-virtual-trial.pdf

Mulcahy, L., Rowden, E., & Tsalapatanis, A. (2022). *Supporting Online Justice: Enhancing Accessibility, Participation and Procedural Fairness.* https://ora.ox.ac.uk/objects/uuid:63fe7b82-d27a-494b-85fc-a146c33822c8

National Audit Office. (2023). *Progress on the Courts and Tribunals Reform Programme* (HC 1130). https://www.nao.org.uk/wp-content/uploads/2023/02/progress-on-courts-and-tribunals-reform-programme-1.pdf

Pleasence, P., Balmer, N. J., & Denvir, C. (2017). Wrong About Rights: Public Knowledge of Key Areas of Consumer, Housing and Employment Law in England and Wales. *The Modern Law Review, 80*(5), 836–859.

Procopiuck, M. (2018). Information Technology and Time of Judgment in Specialized Courts: What Is the Impact of Changing from Physical to Electronic Processing? *Government Information Quarterly, 35*(3), 491–501. https://doi.org/10.1016/j.giq.2018.03.005

Rabinovich-Einy, O. (2008). Beyond Efficiency: The Transformation of Courts Through Technology. *UCLA Journal of Law and Technology, 12*(1), 1–45.

Rabinovich-Einy, O. (2022). Process Pluralism in the Post-COVID Dispute Resolution Landscape. *Texas A&M Law Review, 10*(1), 55–74.

Robinson, J., & Lewis, M. (2020, May 29). Open Justice in Australia: A Silver Lining to the COVID-19 Cloud? *Doughty Street Chambers.* https://insights.doughtystreet.co.uk//post/102g8dq/open-justice-in-australia-a-silver-lining-to-the-covid-19-cloud

Rock, P. (1993). *The Social World of an English Crown Court: Witnesses and Professionals in the Crown Court Centre at Wood Green.* Oxford University Press.

Rossner, M. (2021). Remote Rituals in Virtual Courts. *Journal of Law and Society, 48*(3), 334–361. https://doi.org/10.1111/jols.12304

Rossner, M., & Tait, D. (2023). Presence and Participation in a Virtual Court. *Criminology & Criminal Justice, 23*(1), 135–157. https://doi.org/10.1177/17488958211017372

Rossner, M., Tait, D., McKimmie, B., & Sarre, R. (2017). The Dock on Trial: Courtroom Design and the Presumption of Innocence. *Journal of Law and Society, 44*(3), 317–344. https://doi.org/10.1111/jols.12033

Ryder, E. (2016, March 3). *5th Annual Ryder Lecture: The University of Bolton. 'The Modernisation of Access to Justice in Times of Austerity'.* https://www.judiciary.uk/wp-content/uploads/2016/03/20160303-ryder-lecture2.pdf

SAVE. (2004). *Silence in Court.* SAVE.

Select Committee on the Constitution. (2021). *COVID-19 and the Courts* (HL Paper 257). House of Lords. https://publications.parliament.uk/pa/ld5801/ldselect/ldconst/257/25702.htm

Shapland, J., Willmore, J., & Duff, P. (1985). *Victims in the Criminal Justice System* (pp. 176–178). Gower.

Sturge, G. (2020). *Constituency Data: Magistrates' Court Closures.* https://commonslibrary.parliament.uk/constituency-data-magistrates-court-closures/

Susskind, R. (2021). *Online Courts and the Future of Justice.* Oxford University Press.

Susskind, R. (2023). *Tomorrow's Lawyers: An Introduction to Your Future.* Oxford University Press.

Tait, D. (2018). Rituals and Spaces in Innovative Courts. *Griffith Law Review, 27*(2), 233–253. https://doi.org/10.1080/10383441.2018.1537074

Thomas, R., & Tomlinson, J. (2017). Mapping Current Issues in Administrative Justice: Austerity and the 'More Bureaucratic Rationality' Approach. *Journal of Social Welfare and Family Law, 39*(3), 380–399.

Townend, J., & Magrath, P. (2021). Remote Trial and Error: How COVID-19 Changed Public Access to Court Proceedings. *Journal of Media Law, 13*(2), 107–121. https://doi.org/10.1080/17577632.2021.1979844

Tsalapatanis, A., & Mulcahy, L. (2023). *Designing for Inclusion: How to Produce Inclusive Materials for Advice Sector Clients*. https://ora.ox.ac.uk/objects/uuid:6b1 ddab7-0dca-45ff-be4a-eeffd6bf2a5b

Wallace, A. (2013). Courts and Their Publics: Technology and the Way Forward. In *Australian Courts: Serving Democracy and Its Publics* (pp. 17–37). Australasian Institute of Judicial Administration.

Westermann, H., & Benyekhlef, K. (2023). JusticeBot: A Methodology for Building Augmented Intelligence Tools for Laypeople to Increase Access to Justice. *Proceedings of the Nineteenth International Conference on Artificial Intelligence and Law*, 351–360. https://doi.org/10.1145/3594536.3595166

Wintersteiger, L., Morse, S., Olatokun, M., & Morris, C. J. (2021). *Effectiveness of Public Legal Education Initiatives: A Literature Review*. The Legal Services Board. https://www.legalservicesboard.org.uk/wp-content/uploads/2021/02/PLE-systematic-review-report-Feb-2021.pdf

CHAPTER 4

What Is Lost When Justice Moves Online?

Abstract This chapter considers what is lost when justice moves online. More specifically it addresses the benefits of legal hearings being treated as synonymous with special places, collective ceremonies, rituals, and materiality. The implications of this will be explored in relation to the significance of co-presence, the engendering of a sense of civic occasion, as well as the exercise of State power and its impact on the sensory and psychological quality of interactions. It will reflect on what is lost when the courtroom or hearing room becomes dispersed or transformed into a series of mundane private spaces which people arrive at, and depart from, at the click of a button. The chapter makes two arguments. Firstly, the arrival of online justice heralds a retreat of the State from the civic sphere. Secondly, the shift primarily serves those with political, cultural and social capital, and renders more intense the divide between the digitally empowered and the digitally left behind.

Keywords Courthouse architecture · Online hearings · Journeys to court · Digital disadvantage

INTRODUCTION

Digitalisation is nothing new in the court service. Hybrid hearings are now common and the majority of criminal courts facilitate video appearances by defendants from prison, police stations and NHS psychiatric facilities (Gibbs, 2017). In the civil justice system, the commercial court was an early adopter of video link evidence and many judges and lawyers appear to accept video evidence, especially that given by overseas expert witnesses, as a fairly standard feature of litigation (Hamblen, 2020; Jones, 2017). In the tribunal system the newly launched Video Hearings service is currently being used in tax, property and employment tribunals and tested in civil and family hearings. Fully online and hybrid hearings are now considered by some to be an 'integral part of a twenty-first-century justice system'[1] and there is an expectation that in time, every case will, at the very least, start online (Lord Chancellor et al., 2016). Elsewhere, the Money Claim Online, Divorce Online, Probate Online and the other new platforms mentioned in Table 1.1 in Chapter 1 have been in operation long enough for thousands of people to have used them.

There are many advantages to these innovations and these have been outlined in the last two chapters. But there are also risks which still need to be considered as research and user feedback on the impact of going online emerges. This chapter focuses on detailing these risks. The compact nature of this book means that we have chosen to focus on the shifting dynamics of the delivery of justice caused by the move to online or hybrid hearings. Many of the technological innovations discussed in Chapter 2 might be considered to be equally as revolutionary, but our focus on hearings allows us to move beyond debates about efficiency and speed to consider equally important issues around the transformation of the civic sphere as courthouses disappear from city and town landscapes. We recognise that data on hybrid and fully online hearings is in danger of dating quickly as new, more sophisticated software is developed for use by the courts, the equipment used by the court service is updated and upgraded, and the unusual circumstances in which many trials went online rapidly during the coronavirus pandemic pass (Mulcahy et al., 2020a, 2020b; Ryan et al., 2020; Tomlinson et al., 2020). But underlying these technological innovations the are some fundamental questions about the performance of justice and the value attached to the practice of people still gathering together in a technological age when there are alternatives to doing so.

A key issue which has troubled us as we have written this chapter is whether, in the midst of the intense debate about the advantages and disadvantages of online hearings, there is a danger of losing a broader lens about the political shifts underpinning the modernisation programme. We argue that these need to be viewed in the context of evidence of the retrenchment of the state from the justice system. These include the near abolition of legal aid following the passing of the Legal Aid, Sentencing and Punishment of Offenders Act 2012; the severe rationing of time dedicated to hearings and the equation of case importance with the levels of damages claimed following the Woolf Reforms; increasing pressures to settle out of court through negotiation, mediation or abandonment of claims; severe reductions in the Ministry of Justice budget; and more general evidence of the reduction in the number and proportion of litigated cases that get to a public hearing (Galanter, 2004; Genn, 2009; Mulcahy, 2013). Viewed as part of a package of reforms it could be argued that the shift to online trials can be seen as just another example of the failing faith of the legislature in the importance of citizens asserting their rights. For some, this bundle of initiatives can be seen as part of the legacy of the neo-liberal turn with its focus on a small State, efficiency, consumers and users rather than citizens, and quantifiable effectiveness. In this setting, technological innovation is frequently treated as synonymous with progress and 'modern' can frequently be read as code for cheaper (Ward, 2015). The promises of information technology in reducing costs, improving organisational performance, boosting the efficiency of processes, and accelerating the delivery of public services fit well with this framework (Dumoulin & Licoppe, 2016; but see Dunleavy et al., 2006). Ironically, it is often easier to make the case for increased efficiency when the justice system is constantly being required to perform beyond its capacity (Creutzfeldt, 2021).

There is also a need for other, more pragmatic considerations to be discussed. The Ministry of Justice recognises that hybrid or full online hearings will not always be appropriate, and the decision to have an online hearing remains at the discretion of the judge (Mulcahy & Tsalapatanis, 2022). Despite this safeguard, which allows the judge to take into account the ability and willingness of the parties to proceed online, the question of the sorts of cases which are suitable for online hearings remains to be answered. There is evidence that judicial discretion is being exercised in different ways (Mackeith & Walker, 2011) and it is becoming increasingly clear that the judiciary need to become more experienced in weighing up the risks and benefits of online hearings (Mulcahy & Tsalapatanis, 2022). As we discuss below, this involves a nuanced appraisal of the parties' technological capabilities, the public importance of the case and the need for transparency. In a justice system which is often designed by professional users for professional users, there is a particular need for the social sciences to inform the decision-making process and to explore the experience of online trials from a range of perspectives including, most importantly in the context of this book, those of the laity (Mulcahy & Rowden, 2019).

Against this backdrop, this chapter poses a series of critical questions about the court reform programme. What are the implications of online hearings on conceptions of the courthouse and tribunal building as locally anchored, spatially discrete, and architecturally symbolic? What is lost when the courtroom becomes dispersed or transformed into a series of mundane private spaces from which participants appear? What is the impact of online hearings on the dynamics of adjudication? What design principles from the past do we want to retain in the interest of facilitating participation, dignification and due process in the future? Does the maintenance of a civic landscape in our towns and cities continue to be important to us? Does the trial lose its potency as a public ritual when stripped of its physical surroundings? Is there a danger that techno-evangelicals are too quick to deny fundamental differences which inevitably occur in the transformation from architectural code to video code? Is improving efficiency a sufficient justification for disrupting the dynamics of one of society's most important public events? These questions go to the heart of much more fundamental issues around what renders legal hearings authentic communal or special events. In this chapter, we argue that online hearings are in danger of becoming sanitised, or akin, to just another fleeting encounter mediated by screens.

This chapter is in four main sections. In the first, we begin by discussing the ongoing importance of legal buildings in the civic landscape. The second section considers the significance of journeys to the courtroom in preparing people for hearings and facilitating settlement negotiations. The third section on the shifting dynamics of hearings looks at the impact that online hearings have on the emotional dynamics of interactions and the challenges to open justice. The final section looks at digital disadvantages and the potential of online trials to exclude or undermine the potential for full participation in hearings.

The Role of Buildings in the Civic Landscape

The places in which justice is administered have long played an important part in the civic landscape (Graham, 2003; Mulcahy, 2008, 2011; Resnik & Curtis, 2011). The architecture of the buildings in which hearings take place commonly reflects assumptions that the meting out of justice is a special function of the State and not something which can be dispensed just anywhere or on a whim. Choice of particular sites and the assumption that judges meet with, or visit, the communities they serve at regular intervals are principles that can be traced back to the Magna Carta 1215. Justice has commonly been administered in places, or at times when people are likely to gather such as the agora, the gates of cities, castles, manor houses, moot halls, guildhalls, markets, assembly rooms and public houses (Graham, 2003; Mulcahy, 2011). From the eighteenth century onwards, as custom-built courthouses became common in England, they developed a particular aesthetic which served to reinforce the idea that courthouses are unusual or special places. From this period onwards, law courts were frequently thought of as major commissions of national importance and many were designed by the leading architects of the day. This trend reached its zenith in the nineteenth century when resources were often lavished on monumental, some would say sacral, courthouses which frequently celebrated local trades and achievements through elaborate ornamentation and sculpture (Chase, 2005; Graham, 2003). In England, this was especially evident in the emerging industrial cities of the North of England where the importance of creating a civic landscape of town and city halls, concert halls, reading rooms, art galleries and courthouses became a symbol of the principle of the separation of powers, commercial success, modernity and civic pride (Graham, 2003; Mulcahy, 2011).[2]

The importance of buildings as symbols of the importance of law in the civic landscape is reflected in the fact that the focus of architects responsible for the design of law courts has frequently been on the exterior of the building rather than the organisation of the interior. This signifies the importance placed on law courts having a strong presence in town and cityscapes by those commissioning works. At a practical level, prominent and legible buildings are easier for those using them to find. At a more fundamental level, they are symbols of identity, or civic ideals of fairness, service and the rule of law. Civic buildings, of which law courts have traditionally been an important category, define and shape cities; providing a lens through which they are imagined and governed (Collins, 2016; Dovey, 2009). In this way the exterior of the court building reminds all citizens, regardless of whether they ever have cause to enter it, that law and the legal system are central to the ways in which the modern state is understood.

Conceptions of the role of law in society and architectural styles may change over time, but the argument that buildings communicate important messages about prevailing ideologies continues to be important. This is clear from the fact that court buildings have often been used to signify important shifts in legal, social and political regimes. By way of example, the German Federal Constitutional Court, built in the aftermath of the horrors of the Third Reich, and Antwerp Palais de Justice built after scandals involving judicial corruption, both make extensive use of glass to symbolise a new focus on transparency (Bürklin et al., 2004; Mulcahy & Rowden, 2019). The design of other courts reflects an attempt to acknowledge and move away from histories of colonisation. For example, the metaphor of the tree in the Constitutional Court in South African, built after the abolition of apartheid, reflects a focus on indigenous jurisprudence and indigenous sites for the administration of justice (Le Roux, 2006). The court at Port Augusta in Australia, which is exposed to the elements, makes a similar attempt to demonstrate respect for the settings in which aboriginal justice had traditionally taken place (Mulcahy & Rowden, 2019).

In an English and Welsh context, an analysis of the Court Standards and Design Guides, produced by a consortium of government departments since the 1970s, reflects a shift towards a simpler, accessible aesthetic for exteriors; a move away from baroque and gothic designs which placed emphasis on drama, awe, and the promotion of fear (Mulcahy & Rowden, 2019). A recent edition of the HMCTS Courts and Tribunal Design Guide produced in 2019 continues to acknowledge that court buildings must reflect the dignity and authority of the legal system and 'recognise it as a place where justice is served' (p. 12). More specifically, it requires that court and tribunal buildings are seen as the setting for hearings and a physical statement of the presence and importance of justice. More particularly, it is argued that:

> The appearance of the building itself contributes to perceptions of the role and significance of the court hearing or tribunal. Users' perception and experience of court and tribunal buildings begin from arrival at the entrance to the court or tribunal building. (p. 13)[3]

Earlier versions of the Guide have been even more forceful in reiterating the importance of materiality:

> Court buildings need to be seen to be there and seen to be public, authoritative and important in society, whether an individual has reason to use them or not. Unlike our other buildings, therefore, court buildings cannot be hidden away on an industrial estate or be anonymous suburban office buildings nor can they be seen to be high security compounds or visually oppressive. (Lord Chancellor's Department, 1985)

Despite these authoritative statements, opportunities for buildings and architecture to engender a sense of the civic is clearly diminishing. The extensive court closures discussed in Chapter 1 mean that courthouses are increasingly being demolished or re-purposed. Those that remain are more likely to be positioned in major towns and transport hubs as the idea of local justice becomes an ever more outdated concept. The shift to online hearings and digitalisation further obviates the need for citizens to visit those courthouses that remain. The contribution that such policies make to a diminishing sense of civic or public space has not been lost on social geographers. Not only are public spaces becoming more controlled with the advent of the risk society, but they are also increasingly being commodified by private businesses. As courthouses and hearing centres are closed down, retail architecture is becoming increasingly complex, with branding, place marking, and atmosphere increasingly connected to symbolic values rather than need. In an era in which it is becoming progressively harder for people to see and understand where the administration of justice is taking place, retail outlets are also playing an ever more important role in the shared spaces of cities and towns (Karrholm, 2016; Layard, 2010; Low & Smith, 2013).

Viewed on their own, the recent court closures and the digitalisation of the legal process can be seen as a pragmatic response to the problem of how the modernisations of the justice system is to be funded. It seems eminently sensible for public bodies to seek to reduce expenditure where possible, and both the sale of old building stock and digitalisation have considerable potential to reduce running costs and delays. But these developments also have to be set against other broader debates about the dematerialisation of civic landscapes and the future of town and city centres, many of which are already at risk from out of town retail parks. By contrast with the seeming spacelessness of the internet, we argue that public buildings such as law courts should be seen as more than service delivery centres. We contend that a physically conceived public realm, with justice centres in their heart, remains of ongoing importance to communities; distinguishing them from commercial or social spaces.

JOURNEYS TO THE COURT

Court buildings also play an important role in preparing people for hearings; helping them to transition from the mundane environment of everyday life to a special environment befitting the importance of their interaction with the legal system. Journeys from the outside world, through the courthouse to the courtroom serve to reinforce the fact that appearing before a judge is not an ordinary or everyday experience; they provide a time for reflection and adjustment. Recognising this, the Courts and Tribunal Design Guide (HMCTS, 2019) requires that courthouse design should be thought of as a sequence of major internal spaces which logically lead the public from the main entrance to the waiting areas and to the hearing rooms. Architects commonly acknowledge the importance of these journeys by presenting court users with a series of spaces characterised as the threshold, entrance hall, waiting for area, ante chamber and courtroom. These subtle transitions are not possible in online hearings in which participants are transported from the comfort of a home or office into a virtual courtroom at the click of a mouse pad.

Courts are commonly set back from highways in ways that provide a threshold or transition zone. These threshold spaces engender a sense of movement from the everyday hustle and bustle of the highway to the rarefied interior of the courthouse (see further Karmi-Melamede, 1990). Those approaching the court are forced to make a crossing, to quit the everyday world as they approach the tension point of the entrance (Rock, 1993). The sense of entering a special building is critical to this and an aspiration which is reflected in the advice to architects provided by the Courts and Tribunal Design Guide (2019) which requires that:

> Particular attention should be paid to the main entrance. Its proportions should reflect the size and importance of the court and tribunal building and provide a civic presence to reflect the status of the law in society. Respect for the law and decisions made within the building should be conveyed by the building. (p. 72)

A variety of devices have been used over time to create the sensation of stepping over a threshold including generous entrance halls, steps leading to the door of the courthouse or hearing centre, the prominent display of a court of arms or statues of Justitia.

Having entered the courthouse or hearing centre, court users progress through security into what is commonly a large-scale entrance hall, or salle de pas perdu. HMCTS (2019) require that these entrances should be spacious and set the tone for the user's experience of the court and tribunal building. This includes an expectation that they will act as information hubs where a reception, clear signage and wayfinding can be used to guide all users to their destination. These entrance halls have also traditionally housed public counters where forms can be picked up, documents deposited, and payments made. From the entrance hall, court users progress to waiting areas near the court they will be appearing in, or to consultation rooms where litigants and witnesses can talk to lawyers. Taken together these spaces are intended to play an essential role in helping users to acclimatise themselves and prepare for their hearing (HMCTS, 2019).

Transitional spaces in the courthouse or hearing centre serve other functions, not least of which are the opportunities for informal exchange of information, impromptu settlement negotiations, or fact checking between the reporters and the barristers and court staff (Select Committee on the Constitution, 2021; Ward, 2015). Public counters, now replaced by regional call centres or webchat, have traditionally served an important function in providing opportunities for court staff to advise litigants about which forms they need to use or to draw attention to mistakes they might have made. Face-to-face contact of this kind was particularly important for vulnerable users of the legal system. The recent centralisation of such support in service centres with no local connections has been widely criticised as providing a much poorer service to unrepresented litigants in need of in-person support, and there have been recent calls in research commissioned by HMCTS to re-open information centres in courts (Hanrahan, 2021).

The change to centralised advice administered over the phone or online has been seen as a shift to a transactional model of engagement in which citizens become customers. 'Innovations' of this kind are frequently based on models taken from the private sector where the primary motivation is profit and efficiency. Platform capitalism adds to this trend by its marginalisation of the importance of a physical estate (Srnicek, 2017). Research on telephone advice suggests that outcomes can vary significantly (Smith et al., 2013) and that telephone advice might take longer to deliver (Balmer et al., 2012). It also remains the case in the public sector that local knowledge, networks, and a personal approach to service delivery remain critical. Call centre staff are seen as lacking sufficient experience in how hearings work to be able to ask all the questions posed (Burton, 2018). Research has also shown that the provision of telephone advice challenges the long history of association between social welfare law advice and local delivery within disadvantaged communities. This means that familiarity with the geographical location, knowledge of local policies and procedures, relationships with opponents and allies, and an understanding of the 'local legal culture' is lost and those seeking to assert their rights are less well served. A report on digital support services commissioned by HMCTS has also shown that local contacts and advice services remain vital in the process of referring clients to centralised services (The Good Things Foundation, 2020). Moreover, the police have also argued that engagement with local court staff in the victim and witness issues can frequently ensure and effective hearing (Select Committee on the Constitution, 2021).

Sitting outside of a hearing room in the waiting area can also serve an important function. Court users can enter waiting rooms in physical courthouses whenever they choose to, watch the flow and rhythm of activity, and pick up vital cues about the role of the usher in choreographing proceedings so that everyone is in the right place at the right time. Questions can also be asked of court staff about the likely start time of the hearing they are there to attend. As any court ethnographer knows, it is the usher, clerks and administrative staff within a courtroom that frequently help to orient visitors and introduce them to the conventions of the place. By way of contrast, those attending online trials are frequently told not to enter virtual spaces until 30 minutes (and often less) before the hearing is due to take place. When they do enter the virtual hearing room there is nothing to do but wait, watch a screen, and prepare for an immediate and unceremonial entrance into the virtual hearing.

INSIDE THE HEARING ROOM: THE SHIFTING DYNAMICS OF HEARINGS

Once inside the hearing room, a number of issues have been raised by researchers about the ways in which online presence impacts on the dynamics of the proceedings. The first of these relates to the placing of people in space. Depending on the platform being used, online hearings commonly present participants on a grid, with the arrangement of faces on screen often dictated by the order in which participants enter the online meeting.[4] Much more extensive thought, spanning hundreds of centuries, has been given to the minutiae of how the various participants in a trial are positioned in relation to each other (Graham, 2003; Mulcahy, 2011). More recently, the Court Standards and Design Guide contain complex specifications which prescribe in considerable detail how the internal space of all courthouses should be configured and space allocated. These guides inform us of such things as the correct height, width, and depth of the witness box; the height of the judicial dais; positioning of the public, jury, lawyers, clerks, ushers, transcribers, probation officers and social workers in relation to each other and the positioning of doors. More particularly they have prescribed how the 'sightlines' of each participant should be managed and outline expectations about who should be able to see whom clearly. Though criticised (see Mulcahy & Rowden, 2019) these specifications do, at least, reveal the care with which government ministries, the judiciary and the legal profession have determined the placing of bodies in space. By way of contrast Cloud Video Platform, the first video hearings programme used by HMCTS, was widely criticised for its failure to get these issues right (Byrom et al., 2020).

This accumulated wisdom is rendered redundant when the space in which hearings take place becomes distributed across a series of mundane and domestic spaces rarely designed with a civic purpose in mind. Rather than the State choosing the setting from which evidence is given or the trial viewed, this decision is given over to others. Little attention to date has been paid to whether participants in virtual hearings feel comfortable in such close virtual proximity to others, or want people with whom they are in dispute, in their home or office via their computer. In some instances, the location from which people appear cannot be chosen. This is the case when people appear from institutional or coercive settings (Rossner, 2021). In a video link pilot scheme in Kent launched in 2009, defendants appeared in courts from police stations and it is also common for people to appear from prisons or hospitals when they are on remand or being detained against their will (Terry et al., 2010). Carolyn McKay's (2015, 2018) work on the subjective and sensorial experiences of prisoners who appeared in court via video link from prison in Australia is important in this context. She draws attention to the ways in which background noises, or what she calls a soundtrack of incarceration, infiltrates into the prison video studio and then the virtual courtroom, alerting others to the fact that the prisoner is detained.

The importance of architecture and design is frequently marginalised, if not completely denied in online hearings. Researchers have drawn attention to the careless way in which court-based video suites for vulnerable witnesses are designed, with insufficient attention being paid to such things as the sort of backdrop that might render the defendant dignified. Commenting on the sometimes chaotic backdrops that appear in online hearings, Rossner (2021) has asked whether it is really appropriate for the judge to see someone's spare duvet in the course of proceedings (see also Mulcahy et al., 2020a). As with any backdrop, it has been argued that what is visible behind the remote participant and how they are framed by the camera, requires careful consideration to ensure that the tone is comparable to an in-person court appearance. In some instances, poor lighting, camera placement and awkward angles can create poor visibility leading to additional difficulty in reading reactions, non-verbal cues, and demeanour (Rowden, 2011, 2018; Rowden & Wallace, 2018). By way of example, the Bail Observation Project has observed that poor lighting can mean that it is more difficult to distinguish the features of a person appearing via video link who has dark skin (MacKeith & Walker, 2013). Appearing from one's home can also be a problem for the impoverished, forced to appear online from the chaos of a crowded bedsit in which it is difficult to find an appropriate place close to a strong internet connection to act as a frame (Mulcahy et al., 2022). Existing protocols are silent on the issue of how, and indeed whether, the facilities used by participants should be suitable for the function asked of them.

There is also evidence that litigants and defendants appearing online in hybrid hearings face barriers in developing and maintaining a relationship with their lawyer (Select Committee on the Constitution, 2021). In some instances, this is because time spent with a lawyer is more strictly rationed in online proceedings (Mackeith & Walker, 2013). Research undertaken by Licoppe and Dumoulin (2010) has also drawn attention to the new dilemmas faced by lawyers whose clients appear by video link when others are gathered in a courtroom (see also Terry et al., 2010). They found that lawyers are unclear whether they are best able to protect the interests of their clients by travelling to sit with them in their video suite, or by appearing in the court where they feel they might have more opportunities to influence the judge.[5] Fielding et al. (2020) also found that the loss of face-to-face contact in video court can create challenges in terms of advocates developing trust and rapport with their clients In a similar vein, the Ministry of Justice video-enabled hearings pilot conducted in 2009–2010 in Kent, found that the physical separation of defendants and their solicitors made it harder for defence and CPS lawyers to communicate before and during hearings (Terry et al., 2010).

Looking at the trial from the perspective of a performance artist, Radul (2007) has offered some important insights into the ways in which live performances in traditional courtrooms might differ from those undertaken online. For her, the screen places a barrier of glass between the participants that produce a dialectic of inclusion-exclusion, presence-absence, and divider-connective; interactions become 'talking heads' and torsos behind glass at the expense of the whole body. Viewed in this way, online hearing can be seen to promote cognitive confusion and complexity by creating physically separate but connected spaces. In a similar vein, several commentators have argued that video link made appearing in court 'unreal' or 'impersonal' (Plotnikoff & Woolfson, 1999, 2000), and other research suggests that lay participants have difficulty understanding what is going on (see also Jacobson et al., 2015). The Select Committee on the Constitution argued in 2021 that:

> Attending court can be a stressful and alienating experience. The outcome of a court case can be life-changing for the individuals involved. That is true of many family, employment and asylum cases where emotions run high and users' perceptions of fairness are fragile. Remote technology heightened these challenges in a number of ways. Early reports on the use of remote hearings in the family courts found that a lack of face to face contact during audio and video hearings made it "extremely difficult" to conduct hearings with an appropriate level of empathy and humanity. As one judge put it "[t]he court process is more important than simply being an administrative adjudication. It's a very human set of interactions". This risked alienating court users and undermining public faith in court processes. (paras 87–88)

Ryan et al.'s (2020) empirical study of the use of online hearings in the family courts during the pandemic found that many respondents found it difficult to engage in remote hearings with the level of empathy and humanity that is required (see also Rossner, 2021). Increased levels of tiredness from constant working on screen have also reported; with people complaining that the level of concentration required at online or telephone interactions and the feeling of additional exposure to the scrutiny of others is much more intense (see also Select Committee on the Constitution, 2021). These findings raise critical concerns about the propensity of online encounters to facilitate a sense of emotional distance rather than effective participation. It seems likely that this will impact assessments of procedural justice (Lind & Tyler, 1988); affecting people's perceptions of whether they have been genuinely listened to or treated fairly.

Scholars have argued that new ways of imagining online trials, online rituals and creating a sense of gravitas need to be urgently debated and addressed in judicial training. The introduction of video conferencing technologies in courts also has the potential to have a profound, and potentially transformative affect, on the production, management, and consumption of judicial authority (Rossner, 2021). By way of example, Rowden (2018) has reported a sense of loss of identity among judges who use video technology. In a three-year empirical study of the use of video links in Australian courts, Rowden and Wallace (2018) also found that judges were required to do more in online trials including needing to confirm the identity of those participating in the trial, ensure that documents are visible, undertake courtroom orientation exercises, make sure witnesses were not being harassed or bullied in their remote location which involves picking up subtle cues online (see also Wallace et al., 2019). Other research has found that turn-taking conventions needed to be more explicitly signposted (Rossner & McCurdy, 2018).

Researchers have also drawn attention to the loss of numerous rituals in online trials such as standing when the judge enters the court or the convention of lawyers bowing to the court when they enter and leave; both of which centre on the authority of the judge (see for example Tait, 2018). In the words of Rowden and Wallace (2018) '[i]f architecture sets the scene, court rituals punctuate the message and reinforce the point' (p. 515). Attention has been drawn in this context to the much-neglected topic of the importance of camera angles, lighting, backdrop and relative size of the judge when endangering a sense of prestige for the judge in online hearings (Mulcahy et al., 2020a, 2020b; Mulcahy & Rowden, 2019; Rowden & Wallace, 2018). In the absence of the judicial canopy, coat of arms and other visual cues about hierarchy in online trials, the task of making clear the importance and authority of the judge is rendered much more challenging. This is reflected in the fact that some judges and experienced litigants have expressed a concern that lay participants appeared to act in a less formal manner during their video hearings than they would have had they appeared in court (Mulcahy et al., 2020a; Rossner & McCurdy, 2018; Terry et al., 2010). Rowden and Wallace (2018) have also drawn attention to fears that the oath is not taken as seriously when administered online (see also Wallace et al., 2019).

Research by Bowen and Gibbs (2018) has shown that the also public remains ambivalent about the loss of gravitas in online hearings, in all but perfunctory cases. In their words:

> At the risk of seeming old fashioned, are there not some matters which are just too important to leave to a virtual experience? This is not about whether defendants, victims or witnesses prefer to appear in court – it is about whether there is an expectation from the public and therefore a duty on the state to take some matters so seriously that the formality and ritual of a physical court appearance, even if it is an inconvenient, is a necessity. As we have seen in the public polling, the public expect contested hearings to be in a physical

courtroom. It seems, from the public attitudes we have looked at, that a physical court hearing in these cases underline the seriousness with which the state takes both the liberty of the individual and the gravity of the offence. (p. 43)

Comments of this kind are frequently made in relation to the criminal justice system but could equally easily apply to hearings in a civil justice context involving issues in which there is a broader public interest, or a need to reinforce the importance of those in positions of power being called to account. This might include immigration proceedings, medical negligence cases, judicial reviews and cases in which the consumer is challenging a standard clause in a business to consumer contract.

These various issues have led to arguments that certain types of hearing are simply unsuitable for online or hybrid hearings. By way of example, the Magistrates Association has argued that fully video hearings are not appropriate for any cases involving litigants in person, vulnerable parties, cases where children have to attend, or contested hearings (Select Committee on the Constitution, 2021). Though an early adopter of online hearings, criticisms of its use in remand cases have also been especially strong. It is often assumed that preliminary or perfunctory hearings are well suited to online interactions because they save the cost and inconvenience of transporting the accused from a detention centre for a short appearance. However, judges providing evidence to the Select Committee on the Constitution (2021) argued that remand hearings in Magistrates Courts, in which pleas are entered are considered much too complex to conduct effectively online. As the committee reported, remand hearings involve complex case management decisions involving the police, advocates, the CPS, HMCTS, probation services, drug intervention teams and interpreters which pertain to the liberty of people who have been accused but not convicted:

> Remand hearings are some of the most complex in the criminal justice system, occurring at short notice [...] and often within a day or so of the offence having been committed. It is equally important for both the defendant and the criminal justice system that there is the fullest engagement possible between the parties. Decisions at this stage will determine if the (as yet unconvicted) defendant will lose their liberty and also dictate the time and resources needed to progress the case to a conclusion.

Concerns about the shifting dynamics of the trial are far from unimportant for those concerned. Alarms have, for instance, been raised about the differential outcomes when defendants appear on video in hybrid hearings (Select Committee on the Constitution, 2021, but see Ellison & Munroe, 2014; Rossner, 2021). The Bail Observation Project has argued that immigration bail hearings are much more likely to result in a refusal of bail when they are conducted online (Mackeith & Walker, 2013). Others have reasoned that it is easier to do something detrimental to someone when they are not physically present (Gibbs, 2017). The first evaluation of the video link pilot for preliminary hearings and non-trial matters conducted by Plotnikoff and Woolfson (1999), found that 80% of defence lawyers, 20% of defendants, 20% of prosecutors and 10% of Magistrates interviewed felt that the use of live link was unfair. Significantly the Ministry of Justice evaluation of the Kent pilot scheme found that the rate of guilty pleas and custodial sentences was higher in the pilot than in traditional courts, although this might be explained by the fact that the rate of defence representation was also lower in virtual hearings (Terry et al., 2010).

The Threat to Open Justice

The threat of online trials to open justice remains an ongoing concern, and it is fair to say that the complications in rendering justice transparent when hearings are held online or on the telephone have not yet been satisfactorily resolved (Rossner & McCurdy, 2018).[6] The value of open justice hardly needs repeating, suffice to say that publicity can lead to new evidence coming forward, allow the conduct of the judiciary and advocates to be scrutinised, provide opportunities for citizens to learn more about the hearing of the justice system and engender trust in it. But despite the importance of the principle, there are very real practical difficulties in recreating the public gallery in online hearings and these cannot be solved by allowing all 'present' to appear online. Screen-based gatherings with multiple participants can become problematic, making it difficult for participants to identify who is speaking, what the role of everyone is, and who is important.

The first step to open justice is identifying which cases are suitable to be heard online or in a hybrid format. Traditionally, the public has been able to find out what cases are being heard on any given day by attending courts and viewing the lists posted there. HMCTS has announced that it will make lists of forthcoming cases available online, but research conducted during the pandemic revealed that this information can be hard to access, or is made public so late that it can be difficult to plan attendance in advance (Tomlinson et al., 2020). The Courts and Tribunals Design Guide (HMCTS, 2019) suggests that journalists and the public could access online proceedings using observation terminals located in viewing areas inside court buildings. However, it remains unclear how these will operate, how capacity will be managed when there is a high demand from the public to view a particular case, how judges will continue to manage attendance at hearings by those who should not be present, and the increasingly difficult question of information security (Select Committee on the Constitution, 2021). Finally, there are issues about what journalists and the public are able to see through these portals. Court closures also make these observation terminals much less accessible than the viewing galleries have been in the past.

Another solution to the transparency challenge in online hearings has been to record proceedings and make them available to the public. This practice is now common in international courts and the UK Supreme Court and has considerable potential to make proceedings accessible to others in their home where they can watch pre-recorded or livestreamed hearings at their convenience. However, there remains a lack of clarity among those responsible for the modernisation programme about how the principles of open justice are to be enhanced in this way or how members of the public are to be made aware of their rights. At times, there has also been a particular focus on the needs of the media without broadening the debate about direct access for citizens (Byrom et al., 2020). This is particularly worrying given concerns that members of the public now have to request access to online hearings when all that was necessary in the past was for them to walk into court. The declining presence of journalists in all but the most sensational cases also renders reliance on professionals reporting trials in the newspapers problematic. Even more worrying have been the ways in which lack of activity in promoting transparency has been justified on the basis that members of the public might abuse their position as online observers by recording hearings on the suggestion that the press are adequate proxies (Select Committee on the Constitution, 2021). In light of these criticisms, concerns have been raised that transparency appears to be a secondary consideration in the drive for modernisation.[7]

Digital Disadvantage

The concerns rehearsed above are particularly acute in online hearings involving vulnerable participants, such as those experiencing mental health problems, language and literary barriers, substance dependency, homelessness or poverty. Other vulnerabilities such as youth, learning difficulties or autism may also be hidden and more difficult to identify online than in person where there are more opportunities for informal encounters before, during and after the hearing (Select Committee on the Constitution, 2021). In the words of Gibbs (2017):

> Alarm bells are ringing particularly loud about the use of video for people with mental health problems, learning disabilities, and autism. It can be hard to recognise when a defendant has a disability or support needs when they appear in court in person, and it is harder still when they appear on video. (p. 2)

There have been calls for future developments to include a strategy for identifying and addressing user vulnerabilities and a minimum standard of resilience that lay users need to meet in order to participate in a video hearing instead of an in-person hearing (Mulcahy et al., 2020a, 2020b; Mulcahy & Tsalapatanis, 2022; Rossner & McCurdy, 2018). Rossner and McCurdy's (2018) evaluation of online hearings in the Tax chamber found that the video hearings administration team played a vital role in providing support to lay participants in hearings (see also Mulcahy et al., 2020a) but there appear to be issues about whether HMCTS are willing or able to maintain this level of support (Rossner & McCurdy, 2018). Gibbs (2017) has argued that to make the system fit for purpose for all involved would cost millions of pounds that the Ministry of Justice does not have.

Digitalisation and the shift to online trials also brings with it a risk that a significant proportion of the population will be excluded from the modernised justice system because of their lack of access to equipment or broadband (Allmann, 2022; JUSTICE, 2018; ONS, 2019). It has been argued that insufficient attention has been paid by reformers or the judiciary to the issue of how to accommodate the digitally disadvantaged in the age of online trials (Mulcahy & Tsalapatanis, 2022). Estimates suggest that 6.3% of UK adults have never used the internet (ONS, 2021) and that almost a third (29%) of the population has low digital engagement, with 2.6 million people in the UK still being offline (Lloyds Bank, 2021a). Moreover, 19% of the population lack even foundation level essential digital skills when they do use the internet (Lloyds Bank, 2021b).

In a legal context, Pleasence et al.'s (2015) analysis of the English and Welsh Civil and Social Justice Panel Survey data found that only about 25% of those facing legal problems made use of the internet but in line with other studies, they surmised that access to broadband at home and higher levels of education were the most reliable predictors of use. Denvir et al.'s (2021) research into digital skills in the legal arena demonstrated that while the disadvantaged may have the skills to go online, they are not as effective as the advantaged in using the internet to find *relevant* legal information. It is also the case that even among frequent users of the internet we are beginning to see examples of narrow use and device limited literacy (Allmann, 2022).

There is no national data published by the Ministry of Justice or HMCTS on the number of online video hearings, but the information that is available suggests that during the pandemic litigants attending in-person hearings were *slightly* more likely than those in online hearings to be identified as having additional support needs (Clark, 2021, but see Ryan et al., 2020). However, the proportion of people identified is low in comparison with the national profile. The disparity becomes even more evident when one takes into account that those most likely to be digitally disadvantaged, such as the poor and people with learning or mental health difficulties, are overrepresented in some sections of the legal system such as the criminal courts, social security and child support tribunals. In a civil law context, doubt has been raised about the ability of members of the judiciary to judge when a case is suitable for trial and the lack of training in how to spot vulnerabilities when the cues are subtle (Mulcahy & Tsalapatanis, 2022). Particular concerns have been raised about the extent to which the digital-first agenda being promoted by the government means that the laity is being coerced into an online hearing. In the case of some police station-court links, it has been contended that all defendants are now automatically booked to appear on video from the police station and that the most recent Criminal Procedure Rules suggest judges should always opt for video hearings, except when the defendant is actually on trial (Gibbs, 2017).

Online hearings require a range of digital skills commonly involving a number of complex abstract steps (Allmann & Blank, 2021). Research suggests that anxieties can arise as a result of litigants having to access unfamiliar technology and that this can exacerbate the existing stress involved in having to go to court. Moreover, these factors can deter people from speaking or asking questions (Gibbs, 2017; MacKeith & Walker, 2011). Problems of this kind could be alleviated with pre and post-hearing explanations or support but, as has already been suggested above, this is not always available (Ryan et al., 2020). The implications of this are stark when one considers that existing guidance on joining an online hearing variously requires litigants: to install or test their ability to participate in the hearing; maintain a stable connection and minimum bandwidth; share files; use a side panel for messaging; mute their microphones; have an electronic device with camera, speaker and microphone and ideally a second one to navigate the bundle (Mulcahy & Tsalapatanis, 2022). These challenging minimum requirements have the capacity to further alienate those who are already at the margins of technical competence and confidence.

In their survey of court clerks, ushers and interpreters Mulcahy and Tsalapatanis (2022) found that problems with people participating in online hearings which were commonly cited included people not being able to log in, not being able to navigate the controls once a hearing had started, using the mute function when speaking, lack of access to a reliable broadband, poor bandwidth, and not being able to access a desktop, laptop, tablet or even a smartphone. Where the disadvantaged could access a suitable device to appear from it was not uncommon for it to be a smartphone. Indeed, recent research undertaken by HMCTS showed that the top three devices used by public users attending remote hearings were mobile phones (61%), laptops (21%) and landline phones (10%) (Clark, 2021). Accessing an online hearing using a small screen clearly makes the gap between the ideal conditions of an in-person trial and online justice even greater, with facial expressions and cues even harder to read and the sound quality poorer than would be the case if using a desktop.

Conclusion

The issues raised in this chapter touch upon both pragmatic and philosophical concerns about the direction in which technology is taking the justice system. On the one hand, the rapid closure of courts in recent years has caused considerable consternation among professional groups and the advice sector. Ironically, these court closures are being used to fund online justice initiatives before their value as alternatives to face-to-face hearings have been established. At the same time, the longer journeys to face-to-face hearings that people are now having to undertake are likely to make online alternatives more attractive. Various commentators have urged governments to delay their plans for video hearings until they have commissioned more research and come to a clearer appreciation of the impact of online hearings on decision-making (Dumoulin & Licoppe, 2016; Rossner & McCurdy, 2018; Select Committee on the Constitution, 2021). As this chapter demonstrates, social scientists have an extremely important role to play in debates about what is lost when justice goes online. The studies discussed make clear the importance of taking traditional notions of ritual; ceremony, traditional notions of presence and gathering seriously in an information age.

The chapter also raises more fundamental issues about the way that society perceives and evidences its commitment to the justice system. In an era of austerity, attempts on the part of the government to achieve efficiencies in the administration of justice are clearly laudable and it has not been the intention of this chapter to undermine the importance of this agenda. There are undoubtedly many failings in the administration of justice which need to be addressed including delays, frequent adjournment of cases, bewildering procedures, inaccessibility and the attention paid to the needs of lay users. The arguments made in this chapter do however suggest that reform of the justice system should not be driven solely by the need for greater efficiency. Maintaining and nurturing a sense of the civic sphere remains important, if not essential, in a post-democratic era in which the chasm between rich and poor is increasing. It is relevant in this context that many citizens feel unconnected with those who govern and run state institutions (Crouch, 2004) and that there is a growing need to reconnect with the concept of public life or sense of community (Crouch, 2004; Sennett, 1977) rather than focusing on the dispersal of public spaces. Moving beyond the economics of justice reform, this chapter has sought to encourage discussions of the sociology, anthropology and psychology of encounters with the legal system to the fore.

Notes

1. https://insidehmcts.blog.gov.uk/2021/06/09/remote-hearings-their-role-in-extending-access-to-justice/. See also Rossner (2021).
2. Examples include Manchester Assize Court, Victoria Law Courts in Birmingham, St. George's Hall in Liverpool, the courts at Leeds Town Hall, Durham Crown Court, Devizes Assize Courts, Beverley Guildhall, and Bedford Shire Hall.
3. To access a copy of this guide see: https://www.gov.uk/government/publications/court-and-tribunal-design-guide.
4. The new video hearings system now being rolled out allows the judge to choose the format and 'pin' particular people.
5. See further https://www.lawgazette.co.uk/practice/virtual-court-pilot-is-not-fit-for-purpose/5057884.article.
6. This has led to the Select Committee on the Constitution (2021) to recommend that the senior judiciary convene a working group to protect and enhance media access to proceedings.

7. Gibbs (2017) has for instance argued that the principles of open justice has been seriously compromised by the introduction of the Single Justice Procedure. This allows pleas to be entered online and for defendants to be sentenced on the basis of documents submitted to a closed court.

BIBLIOGRAPHY

Allmann, K. (2022). *UK Digital Poverty Evidence Review*. Digital Poverty Alliance.

Allmann, K., & Blank, G. (2021). Rethinking Digital Skills in the Era of Compulsory Computing: Methods, Measurement, Policy and Theory. *Information, Communication & Society, 24*(5), 633–648.

Balmer, N. J., Smith, M., Denvir, C., & Patel, A. (2012). Just a Phone Call Away: Is Telephone Advice Enough? *Journal of Social Welfare and Family Law, 34*(1), 63–85.

Bowen, P., & Gibbs, B. (2018). *Just Technology: Emergent Technologies and The Justice System. And What the Public Thinks About It*. London Centre for Justice Innovation.

Bürklin, T., Limbach, J., & Wilkens, M. (2004). With a Touch of Internationality and Modernity. *The Federal Constitutional Court of Germany: Architecture and Jurisdiction (Das Bundesverfassungsgericht in Karlsruhe: Architektur und Rechtsprechung)*, 15–42.

Burton, M. (2018). Justice on the Line? A Comparison of Telephone and Face-to-Face Advice in Social Welfare Legal Aid. *Journal of Social Welfare and Family Law, 40*(2), 195–215.

Byrom, N., Beardon, S., & Kendrick, A. (2020). *The Impact of COVID-19 Measures on the Civil Justice System*. The Legal Education Foundation. https://discovery.ucl.ac.uk/id/eprint/10107392/1/CJC-Rapid-Review-Final-Report-f.pdf

Chase, O. G. (2005). *Law, Culture, and Ritual: Disputing Systems in Cross-Cultural Context*. NYU Press.

Clark, J. (2021). *Evaluation of Remote Hearings During the COVID Pandemic* (Research Report). HMCTS. https://assets.publishing.service.gov.uk/government/uploads/system/uploads/attachment_data/file/1040183/Evaluation_of_remote_hearings_v23.pdf

Collins, T. (2016). Urban Civic Pride and the New Localism. *Transactions of the Institute of British Geographers, 41*(2), 175–186.

Creutzfeldt, N. (2021). Towards a Digital Legal Consciousness? *European Journal of Law and Technology, 12*(3). https://www.ejlt.org/index.php/ejlt/article/view/816

Crouch, C. (2004). *Post-Democracy*. Polity.

Denvir, C., Sutherland, C., Selvarajah, A., Balmer, N., & Pleasence, P. T. (2021). *Access to Online Courts: Exploring the Relationship Between Legal and Digital Capability*. https://doi.org/10.2139/ssrn.3838153

Dovey, K. (2009). *Becoming Places: Urbanism/Architecture/Identity/Power*. Routledge.

Dumoulin, L., & Licoppe, C. (2016). Videoconferencing, New Public Management, and Organizational Reform in the Judiciary. *Policy & Internet, 8*(3), 313–333.

Dunleavy, P., Margetts, H., Bastow, S., & Tinkler, J. (2006). New Public Management Is Dead—Long Live Digital-Era Governance. *Journal of Public Administration Research and Theory, 16*(3), 467–494.

Ellison, L., & Munro, V. E. (2014). A 'Special' Delivery? Exploring the Impact of Screens, Live-Links and Video-Recorded Evidence on Mock Juror Deliberation in Rape Trials. *Social & Legal Studies, 23*(1), 3–29.

Fielding, N., Braun, S., Hieke, G., & Mainwaring, C. (2020). *Video Enabled Justice Evaluation*. Sussex Police and Crime Commissioner and University of Surrey. http://spccweb.thco.co.uk/media/4851/vej-final-report-ver-11b.pdf

Galanter, M. (2004). The Vanishing Trial: An Examination of Trials and Related Matters in Federal and State Courts. *Journal of Empirical Legal Studies, 1*(3), 459–570.

Genn, H. (2009). *Judging Civil Justice*. Cambridge University Press.

Gibbs, P. (2017). *Defendants on Video-Conveyor Belt Justice or a Revolution in Access?* Transform Justice.

The Good Things Foundation. (2020). *HMCTS Digital Support Service: Implementation Review*. https://www.goodthingsfoundation.org/insights/hmcts-digital-support-service-implementation-review/

Graham, C. (2003). *Ordering Law: An Architectural and Social History of the English Law Court to 1914*. Aldershot.

Hamblen, L. (2020, October 13). *The Commercial Court: Past, Present, and Future*, Annual Combar Lecture 2020. https://www.supremecourt.uk/docs/speech-201013.pdf

Hanrahan, A. (2021). *Identifying, Understanding, and Responding to the Multiple Complex Needs of Court Service Users*. HMCTS.

HMCTS. (2019). *Courts and Tribunals Design Guide*. https://assets.publishing.service.gov.uk/media/5c9de371ed915d07ae752fef/Court_and_Tribunal_Design_Guide_-_Public_v1.1_-_webOptimised.pdf

Jacobson, J., Hunter, G., & Kirby, A. (2015). *Inside Crown Court*. Policy Press.

Jones, N. (2017). *Video Link Evidence in the Commercial Court: Potential Pitfalls*. https://gatehouselaw.co.uk/video-link-evidence-in-the-commercial-court-potential-pitfalls

JUSTICE. (2018). *Preventing Digital Exclusion from Online Justice*. A Report of JUSTICE. https://files.justice.org.uk/wp-content/uploads/2018/06/06170424/Preventing-Digital-Exclusion-from-Online-Justice.pdf

Karmi-Melamede, A. (1990). *The Supreme Court Building, Israel*. Jerusalem: Perspecta.

Karrholm, M. (2016). *Retailising Space: Architecture, Retail and the Territorialisation of Public Space*. Routledge.

Layard, A. (2010). Shopping in the Public Realm: A Law of Place. *Journal of Law and Society, 37*(3), 412–441.

Le Roux, W. (2006). Bridges, Clearings and Labyrinths: The Architectural Framing of Post-Apartheid Constitutionalism. In *Post-apartheid Fragments* (pp. 59–100). Brill.

Licoppe, C., & Dumoulin, L. (2010). The "Curious Case" of an Unspoken Opening Speech Act: A Video-Ethnography of the Use of Video Communication in Courtroom Activities. *Research on Language and Social Interaction, 43*(3), 211–231.

Lind, E. A., & Tyler, T. R. (1988). *The Social Psychology of Procedural Justice*. Springer Science & Business Media.

Lloyds Bank. (2021a). *UK Consumer Digital Index*. https://www.lloydsbank.com/banking-with-us/whats-happening/consumer-digital-index.html

Lloyds Bank. (2021b). *Essential Digital Skills Report*. https://www.lloydsbank.com/assets/media/pdfs/banking_with_us/whats-happening/211109-lloyds-essential-digital-skills-report-2021.pdf

Lord Chancellor's Department. (1985). *Court Standards and Design Guide*. London, Lord Chancellor's Department.

Lord Chancellor, the Lord Chief Justice and the Senior President of Tribunals. (2016). *Transforming Our Justice System*. https://assets.publishing.service.gov.uk/government/uploads/system/uploads/attachment_data/file/553261/joint-vision-statement.pdf

Low, S., & Smith, N. (Eds.). (2013). *The Politics of Public Space*. Routledge.

MacKeith, B., & Walker, B. (2011). *Immigration Bail Hearings: A Travesty of Justice?: Observations from the Public Gallery*. Campaign to Close Campsfield.

MacKeith, B., & Walker, B. (2013). *Still a Travesty: Justice in Immigration Bail Hearings*. Campaign to Close Campsfield.

McKay, C. (2015). Video Links from Prison: Court "Appearance" Within Carceral Space. *Law, Culture and the Humanities, 14*(2), 242–262.

McKay, C. (2018). *The Pixelated Prisoner: Prison Video Links, Court 'Appearance' and the Justice Matrix*. Routledge.

Mulcahy, L. (2008). The Unbearable Lightness of Being? Shifts Towards the Virtual Trial. *Journal of Law and Society, 35*(4), 464–489.

Mulcahy, L. (2011). *Legal Architecture: Justice*. Routledge.

Mulcahy, L. (2013). The Collective Interest in Private Dispute Resolution. *Oxford Journal of Legal Studies, 33*(1), 59–80.

Mulcahy, L., & Rowden, E. (2019). *The Democratic Courthouse: A Modern History of Design, Due Process and Dignity*. Routledge.

Mulcahy, L., Rowden, E., & Teeder, W. (2020a). *Exploring the Case for Virtual Jury Trials During the COVID-19 Crisis: An Evaluation of a Pilot Study Conducted by JUSTICE*. Available at SSRN 3876199.

Mulcahy, L., Rowden, E., & Teeder, W. (2020b). *Testing the Case for a Virtual Courtroom with a Physical Jury Hub: Second Evaluation of a Virtual Trial Pilot Study Conducted by JUSTICE*. Available at SSRN 3876209.

Mulcahy, L., Rowden, E., & Tsalapatanis, A. (2022). *Supporting Online Justice: Enhancing Accessibility, Participation and Procedural Fairness*. Centre for Socio-legal Studies.

Mulcahy, L., & Tsalapatanis, A. (2022). Exclusion in the Interests of Inclusion: Who Should Stay Offline in the Emerging World of Online Justice? *Journal of Social Welfare and Family Law, 44*(4), 455–476.

ONS. (2019). *Exploring the UK's Digital Divide*. Office for National Statistics. https://www.ons.gov.uk/peoplepopulationandcommunity/householdcharacteristics/homeinternetandsocialmediausage/articles/exploringtheuksdigitaldivide/2019-03-04

ONS. (2021). *Internet Users, UK: 2020: Internet Use in the UK, Annual Estimates by Age, Sex, Disability and Geographical Location*. Office for National Statistics, Statistical Bulletin. https://www.ons.gov.uk/businessindustryandtrade/itandinternetindustry/bulletins/internetusers/2020

Pleasence, P., Balmer, N. J., & Denvir, C. (2015). *How People Understand and Interact with the Law*. The Legal Education Foundation.

Plotnikoff, J., & Woolfson, R. (1999). *Preliminary Hearings: Video Links Evaluation of Pilot Projects*. Final Report. https://www.researchgate.net/profile/Richard-Woolfson/publication/344220066_Preliminary_Hearings_Video_Links_Evaluation_of_Pilot_Projects_Final_Report_Video_Link_Pilot_Evaluation_Contents/links/5f5d0305299bf1d43cfe3d9b/Preliminary-Hearings-Video-Links-Evaluation-of-Pilot-Projects-Final-Report-Video-Link-Pilot-Evaluation-Contents.pdf

Plotnikoff, J., & Woolfson, R. (2000). *Evaluation of Video Link Pilot Project at Manchester Crown Court*. Court Service.

Radul, J. (2007). What Was Behind Me Now Faces Me: Performance, Staging, and Technology in the Court of Law. *Glänta, 1*, 86–98.

Resnik, J., & Curtis, D. E. (2011). *Representing Justice: Invention, Controversy, and Rights in City-States and Democratic Courtrooms*. Yale University Press.

Rock, P. (1993). *The Social World of an English Crown Court: Witnesses and Professionals in the Crown Court Centre at Wood Green*. Oxford University Press.

Rossner, M. (2021). Remote Rituals in Virtual Courts. *Journal of Law and Society, 48*(3), 334–361.

Rossner, M., & McCurdy, M. (2018). *Implementing Video Hearings (Party-to-State): A Process Evaluation*. Ministry of Justice.

Rowden, E. (2011). *Remote Participation and the Distributed Court: An Approach to Court Architecture in the Age of Video-Mediated Communications* (Doctoral dissertation). University of Melbourne, Faculty of Architecture, Building and Planning.

Rowden, E. (2018). Distributed Courts and Legitimacy: What Do We Lose When We Lose the Courthouse? *Law, Culture and the Humanities, 14*(2), 263–281.

Rowden, E., & Wallace, A. (2018). Remote Judging: The Impact of Video Links on the Image and the Role of the Judge. *International Journal of Law in Context, 14*(4), 504–524.

Ryan, M., Harker, L., & Rothera, S. (2020, September). *Remote Hearings in the Family Justice System: Reflections and Experiences*. Nuffield Family Justice Observatory: London.

Select Committee on the Constitution. (2021). *COVID 19 and the Courts, 22nd Report of Session 2019–21* (HL Paper 257).

Sennett, R. (1977). *The Fall of Public Man*. WW Norton & Company.

Smith, M., Balmer, N., Miles, J., & Denvir, C. (2013). In Scope but Out of Reach: Examining Differences Between Publicly Funded Telephone and Face-to-Face Family Law Advice. *Child and Family Law Quarterly, 25*, 253.

Srnicek, N. (2017). *Platform Capitalism*. Wiley.

Tait, D. (2018). Rituals and Spaces in Innovative Courts. *Griffith Law Review, 27*(2), 233–253.

Terry, M., Johnson, S., & Thompson, P. (2010). *Virtual Hearing Pilot Evaluation*. MOJ Research Series 21/10. https://www.justice.gov.uk/downloads/publications/research-and-analysis/moj-research/virtual-courts.pdf

Tomlinson, J., Hynes, J., Marshall, E., & Maxwell, J. (2020) *Judicial Review in the Administrative Court During the COVID-19 Pandemic*. Available at SSRN 3580367.

Wallace, A., Roach Anleu, S., & Mack, K. (2019). Judicial Engagement and AV Links: Judicial Perceptions from Australian Courts. *International Journal of the Legal Profession, 26*(1), 51–67.

Ward, J. (2015). Transforming 'Summary Justice' Through Police-Led Prosecution and 'Virtual Courts' Is 'Procedural Due Process' Being Undermined? *British Journal of Criminology, 55*(2), 341–358.

CHAPTER 5

Conclusion: Towards Inclusive Design

Abstract This final chapter raises a number of issues about different ways of seeing the justice system and technological transformation. Focusing on the needs of the most disadvantaged users of the legal system, we ask a series of questions about the ways in which the mindset of architects of online justice systems and content providers can be seen as biased. The chapter argues that this is due in large part to a failure to take into account the needs and opinions of public users of a public justice system in the design, testing and implementation of online services. Drawing on concepts of participatory design we outline the various ways in which the creation of new knowledge through interacting with the general public constitutes a form of democratic and responsible design.

Keywords Epistemic injustice · Digital government · Participatory research · Digital disadvantage

INTRODUCTION

In this chapter, we raise a number of epistemological issues about ways of seeing the justice system through the lens of inclusive and user-led design. As with other chapters in this book, we approach this topic from the perspective of the most disadvantaged in our society and ask a series of questions about the extent to which the architects of digital transformation have placed the needs of lay users at the centre of the transformation agenda. This issue is of considerable importance as we become increasingly aware that technology is not neutral. Designers and content providers frequently embed their own personal,

© The Author(s), under exclusive license to Springer Nature
Switzerland AG 2024
L. Mulcahy and A. Tsalapatanis, *Digital Justice*, Palgrave Socio-Legal Studies, https://doi.org/10.1007/978-3-031-65265-3_5

cultural and corporate values into the systems they build, with the result that those systems are biased towards certain ways of seeing the world. Negative discrimination can also be developed or amplified over time, as the same information becomes the basis for updated systems. In addition to the problem of bias, the many references to access to justice, modernisation, openness or efficiency made in the course of the debate about reforms in England and Wales reflect different expectations about what the justice system and reforms are intended to achieve based on the standpoint of the person or group from which they are viewed. This makes it important to ask whose ideas and views of the world are being hardwired into digital transformations of the justice system.

Fricker's (2007) concept of epistemic injustice is particularly useful in this context. Defined as a wrong done to someone in their capacity as a knower, she theorises two different categories of epistemic injustice. The first is 'testimonial injustice' which occurs when prejudice causes a hearer to give a deflated level of credibility to a speaker's word. The extent to which testimonial injustice is present in digital reform programmes can be judged according to how often a range of users have been consulted about change and the ways in which that feedback has been responded to or acted upon. The second is hermeneutical injustice which occurs when a gap in collective interpretive resources puts someone at an unfair disadvantage when it comes to making sense of their social experiences. This makes it imperative to recognise that certain individuals may lack the resources or power to define viable categories of experience (Tsosie, 2017) and to design stakeholder processes in ways that account for this. The historical absence of engagement with lay users in the justice system discussed in Chapter 4 raises important questions about the extent to which this historic predisposition has carried over into the era of digital transformations.

In the sections which follow we begin by discussing the extent to which the discourse around digital transformation is being led by private sector ways of thinking, to the detriment of the values of the public sphere. The next section considers in more detail the ways in which the perspectives of lay users have been fed into the design and implementation of the digitalisation programme. The third substantive section turns to suggest how future innovation might be conceived of differently. We argue that despite the rhetoric surrounding current reforms and descriptions of them as radical, that a true transformation involves more fundamental changes in culture relating to how government engages with its citizens.

Digital Government and Digital Business

It is clear from earlier chapters that justice systems have much to learn from the insights offered by the private sector. Private sector involvement in government tasks has been a particularly significant part of public service delivery since the New Public Management initiatives of the 1980s and has increased in popularity following the 2007–2008 global financial crisis (Breaugh et al., 2023; Osei-Kyei & Chan, 2015). In recognition of this, the UK government frequently brings in private sector companies to spearhead design, production and implementation of digital change.[1] There are many benefits to such partnerships including harnessing expertise, risk sharing, flexibility, collaborative governance, and amelioration of infrastructure deficits. Moreover, many of digital dispute resolution processes discussed as exemplars by academics and policymakers have been developed in the private sector albeit with the needs of businesses and consumers in mind.

The notion of public-private partnerships and cross fertilisation of ideas also poses some significant problems in a justice setting. The focus on growth, and competition in the private sector does not fit well with the obligations of the State in the provision of public services; increasing demands for transparency and responsiveness; or the ambition that digitalisation might actually add public value by enhancing citizen engagement and democratic participation. Recognising the wide range of types of public-private partnerships Breaugh et al. (2023) have argued that the bigger the project the more robust stakeholder management and citizen engagement needs to be. In support of this, they argue:

> …when multiple actors with diverse motives participate in public-private partnerships, conflicts between public and private missions can arise, potentially jeopardising the intended impact on end beneficiaries. Furthermore, while measuring private or financial value is relatively straightforward, measuring public values is more complex. (no page number)

As technological expertise in the public sector has fallen behind the private sector, there is also a danger that governments will be outmanoeuvred by the power, know-how and activities of technology companies or management consultants keen to take the lead in diagnosing problems and selling solutions (Fishenden, 2023). Digital transformation of government services is attracting large investments from the public purse which goes some way toward explaining why international companies such as Deloitte which are experts in audit and assurance, consulting, financial advisory, risk advisory and tax, have suddenly become interested in the criminal justice system and virtual prisons (see for example Deloitte, 2021). While there is no doubt that the public and private sectors are dependent upon each other, we argue that it is important for present purposes to consider the distinctive nature of public sector service provision.

Different standards have traditionally been required of government including transparency, accountability, citizen participation and privacy. In part, this is because government is often a monopoly provider. But the differences go deeper. Users are citizens with particular rights, as well as obligations, towards the state rather than 'customers' who can take their custom elsewhere (Contini & Lanzara, 2009, p. 2). The stakes are also much higher when government departments are interacting with citizens in the provision of services. Difficulty in accessing a digitised government system may mean that an individual is not provided with social security benefits or healthcare, or that they cannot apply for or prove their immigration status, pay taxes, or vote in elections. Viewed in this way, the design of online state justice systems has important implications for how e-government is conceived of in democracies (Brewer et al., 2006, p. 473). As Fishenden (2023) has surmised, government services are 'not just about utility, they are also about service, dignity, control and power' (p. ii). Businesses in the private sector may design and promote dispute resolution tools to avoid their use; choosing to bury their dispute resolution policy deep in their website.

It follows, that software developed for the private sector may have a very different way of conceiving transactions with the public. While businesses will want to develop systems which are suitable for, and attractive to their particular client base, government has to take into account the needs of a wide range of very different users. More particularly, they have a duty to provide services which can be accessed by the digitally disadvantaged, neurodiverse, sight or hearing impaired, the disabled, illiterate or those with limited vocabularies or a low reading age. It is worthy of note in this context that nine percent of the UK population do not speak English or Welsh as their main language, that over 16% of adults in England (7.1 million people) have 'very poor literacy skills,' and that the average reading age of people in the UK is just 9 years old (Tsalapatanis & Mulcahy, 2023). Businesses for whom online accounts form a significant proportion of their income do not need, or necessarily have incentives, to respond to the needs of the digitally disadvantaged while the online business remains buoyant. In contrast, government justice systems need to be committed to running offline and online systems in parallel and to support people in the use of the latter, if they are to ensure that everyone has equal access to the system.

The emotional needs of citizens using government e-services may also be radically different to those purchasing a commercial commodity or service online. In addition to the emotional strain involved in pursuing disputes through the justice system, users of government digital services may suffer from situational disadvantage which would not commonly be present in the private sector when purchasing commodities. The term situational disadvantage has been used by the authors to explain the particular, and additional stress, that people may suffer when interacting with government departments which possess the power to deny a benefit, a legal status, incarcerate or fine people. Situational disadvantage may be experienced regardless of educational attainment, familiarity with computer systems or digital skills (Mulcahy & Tsalapatanis, 2022). In line with this, qualitative research on user experiences of the justice system found that in most cases, users' expectations were focused intensely on the outcome of the case, but generally not knowing what to expect intensified anxiety about the process (HMCTS, 2018). The same research found that stress could be further exacerbated by a lack of realistic expectations, such as anticipating an alien environment, or concerns about how they would be treated by staff and judges (see also Hanrahan, 2021).

The implications of this for the design of digital government services are considerable. Engaging with life-altering processes on a computer can be problematic if those designing programmes fail to acknowledge the significance of the dispute being dealt with by those involved. One such example can be found in the work of Hansen and Koefoed Hansen (2022) who explored an online Danish divorce system. Their research found that while the platform was designed well in terms of usability, accessibility and navigating users around legal requirements, it reflected a lack of sensitivity to the emotional and personal experiences of those using it. The authors recount the experience of a participant who struggled with the 'coldness' of the system, especially when encountering the question 'Do you wish to be separated from your spouse?'. She didn't want to be separated from her spouse but it was necessary for her to agree to this question in order to finalise the process.

These various factors mean that attempts to gain insights from private sector dispute systems such as those operated by eBay need to be approached with caution. It can also mean that off-the-shelf commercial software packages are not always suitable for government services. The complexity of designing systems which are fit for use is apparent from the UK experience of designing software for video hearings. A customised off-the-shelf service, Cloud Video Platform, was initially used by HMCTS and rolled out during the pandemic. This had the benefit of avoiding the high costs of designing, testing, and implementing a bespoke system and facilitated speedier implementation. Despite this, the court service has noted their concern that off-the-shelf solutions tend not to pay sufficient attention to the need for the formality, majesty and security of proceedings (HMCTS, 2023a). Cloud Video Platform was implemented in over 150 magistrates' and 70 Crown courts in addition to civil and family jurisdictions in 2020 (Clark, 2021; Fouzder, 2021), but it was not universally liked. Indeed, a survey of judges during the pandemic discovered that it was less popular than other commercial off-the-shelf systems also being utilised. Criticisms included the need for elements that are extremely important in the justice system including larger images of attendees; being able to view all participants on the screen at once; lack of subtitles; lack of integrated private meeting facilities and the need for document sharing facilities (Byrom & Beardon, 2021). Just a few years later a new Video Hearings service was ready for introduction to address these needs and is now working in parallel with CVP, which it will eventually replace.[2] Improvements include greater support in preparing participants for hearings, checks and guidance to ascertain that their equipment is working, explanations of court rules and a monitored hearing network to check connectivity thus ensuring that no one drops out unnoticed.

Engaging the Public

The issues of who designs the systems and their understanding of what makes the public justice system distinctive lead to the issue of whose views inform design. It has been argued that part of the push towards recognising the impact of epistemic justice involves recognising and creating new forms of knowledge, new facts, and new ways of reconciling seemingly incommensurable ways of knowing (Sheller, 2018). A key criticism made of the HMCTS programme of reform has been its failure to consult with the public during the design process. This is a criticism that has been made by both professional groups and those representing the interests of the public. Several witnesses who gave evidence to the House of Commons Justice Committee Report on Reforms (2019) argued that there had not been enough consultation on reform proposals being implemented in England and Wales by HMCTS and this assertion is also reflected in the findings of the House of Commons Public Accounts Committee (2019). More particularly, it was suggested that few avenues were provided for those with 'lived' experience of the court and tribunal system, such as self-represented defendants in housing possession cases or disabled litigants, to contribute to the specification, design or evaluation of new systems. Consultation with the judiciary and legal profession seems to have been more common, but even then was considered insufficient, especially in relation to the introduction of particular schemes. HMCTS 'roadshows' were criticised for not having sufficient capacity or geographical spread to ensure access for a broad range of stakeholders and others complained of closed focus groups or 'lip service' being paid to the need for consultation. HMCTS has since recognised that it must better understand and respond to user concerns (National Audit Office, 2023), but this undertaking has come fairly late in the reform programme.

These reviews of HMCTS performance suggest a general lack of transparency about exactly who has been consulted during the design, testing, and implementation process. While some iterative testing with user groups was used to support the design of new systems, concerns have been raised about the lack of visibility in relation to this exercise. Doubt has also been cast on whether the research conducted into user perspectives had been rigorous enough (House of Commons Justice Committee, 2019). HMCTS claims that in order to properly understand what 'users' want from a modern justice system, they are carrying out an extensive programme of engagement and research.[3] The government website which provides information about the research undertaken or commissioned by HMCTS, has details of nine such research projects. It is significant that all of these have been commissioned *after* a service has been implemented.[4] In a similar vein, the Video Hearings service routinely asks for user feedback at the end of a hearing and provides a link to a survey. Research into the implementation of the new Digital Support system also interviewed members of the public after they had used the service (Good Things Foundation, 2020, 2021).

Small-scale studies of public users' experiences of online services have been undertaken or commissioned by HMCTS (see for instance Clark, 2021; Rossner & McCurdy, 2018) but these remain limited and only one study has focused on public users with complex needs (Hanrahan, 2021). It is sometimes unclear whether engagements with 'stakeholders' or 'court users' include gathering the views of members of the public (HMCTS, 2023b). In other instances, such as online services for those seeking asylum and immigration status, a decision has been made to evaluate the part of the system involving lawyers but not the part that deals with litigants in person (HMCTS, 2022). Finally, references to considering the needs of public users sometimes involve proxies such as those working in the advice sector (see for instance HMCTS, 2020).

At other times there is evidence of testimonial epistemic injustice of the type imagined by Fricker, with the views of certain types of users being prioritised over others. In the first stage of an 'implementation review' conducted by HMCTS May–August 2020, interviews were undertaken with 167 individuals from 'key user groups' which included 59 court staff, 50 judges, 44 legal professionals and 3 support staff. Just 11 or seven percent of the sample was made up of public users (Clark, 2021). Stage two of the HMCTS implementation review took more seriously the need to seek out the views of the public, with 4808 members of the public who had taken part in an online hearing participating in a survey involving 8328 respondents. Additional interviews were undertaken with 78 members of the public. HMCTS reported that some of the challenges raised in the public user interviews were subsequently addressed through iterative service improvements (Clark, 2021).[5] But overall the public has been little involved.

There is even less evidence of HMCTS taking into account the needs of the vulnerable or digitally disadvantaged (but see Hanrahan, 2021). Despite having some important things to say about how decisions about the suitability of an online hearing were made, stage two of the HMCTS evaluation used a sample frame for in-depth interviews which did not include those litigants that the judiciary felt were not able to participate online. Moreover, the push-to-web approach HMCTS adopted for the survey of all users is unlikely to have been conducive to encouraging the digitally disadvantage to take part. It is worthy of note, in this context that the option of a postal survey was withdrawn after a pilot survey because of the low response rate of two percent (HMCTS, 2021), a decision that could well have allowed the views of the digitally disadvantaged to be captured.[6]

In their response to the House of Commons Justice Committee (2019), HMCTS made much of their 'agile' approach to design. 'Agile' as a concept was originally developed by a group of software designers and launched in the Manifesto for Agile Software Development (Agile Software Development, 2001), and is used widely in software and systems development in the UK including by the Government Digital Service.[7] While the iterative design elements associated with this method are useful, it has been criticised due to its focus on speed, and the fact that it allows inadequate time for the types of consultation required to build these systems. It is also worthy of note in this context that the approach has been designed for commercial purposes and may be difficult to adapt to the more rigorous requirements for developing the complicated government services described throughout this book (Misra et al., 2012). The fragmented way in which agile development occurs also makes it difficult to understand the user perspective in terms of a larger end to end journey, and it retains a very narrow and technical focus (Good Things Foundation, 2020).[8] The reform programme has also been criticised by the National Audit Office for not allowing adequate time within their processes to assess what is being designed (National Audit Office, 2018, para. 21a).

There is currently considerable debate in academic circles about how to involve users in research, with an increasing premium being placed on engaging them from the very outset of a co-designed project. Some approaches using his perspective have been criticised for continuing to view users and their needs as objects of study, rather than actual participants in the process (Marti & Bannon, 2009, p. 7). In contrast, it has been argued that good participatory design research conceives of users as partners (Sanders & Stappers, 2008, p. 6), seeking engagement and input at all stages of the research and design process rather than just the testing phase. Different levels or degrees of user involvement such as informing, consulting, collaborating and empowering' (Vaughn & Jacquez, 2020) are possible, but at its core, co-design recognises users as an expert of their own experience (Bobbio, 2019; Sanders & Stappers, 2008). Applying these concepts to a legal context Hagan (2020) has argued that in the nascent field of legal design developed out of work in human-centred and visual design, civic technology, and participatory policy-making:

> ...the craft of legal design is developing as one that combines a community oriented co-design ethos, with a commitment to navigating the bureaucracies of the legal system to effect change, and with the integration of empirical research to evaluate whether user-centered design and policy proposals do, in fact, improve people's outcomes... It brings a lawyerly focus on abstract complexities (e.g., what rights we have, what risks we face, what rules constrain us) with a designerly focus on lived experience (how we do things, how things look and feel to us, how things serve us). Both the lawyerly focus and designerly focus share a core similarity: to strategically improve people's outcomes in a system, to solve complex problems, to be in service. (pp. 3–5)

This approach begins with a phase of seeking to understand a challenge through interviews, ethnography, observations, data gathering and exploratory workshops. This leads to a synthesis of specific user personas, needs statements, requirement lists and design briefs. New ways to resolve problems are explored in brainstorming, speculative designs, collaborative co-design, and early prototyping which slowly move towards specific prototypes, which are tested for usability, experience and feasibility (Hagan, 2020). In his work on participatory research Fletcher recognises a range of different types of knowledge that need to be balanced and configured including academic and formal, experiential, emotional knowledge, systems knowledge and general wisdom (Fletcher, 2023).

These participatory approaches encourage transparency in design, with those in charge having to account for design decisions, as well as responding to various demands and feedback (Mulcahy & Tsalapatanis, 2023). Though challenging to use they can also promote more democratic ways of undertaking research and engaging with citizens by relinquishing control to end-users and mixing up the roles of the user, researcher and designer (Sanders & Stappers, 2008). Unlike 'agile' methodologies, the approach does not assume a singular product owner with a clear vision of what the outcome needs to look like. This makes participatory research particularly valuable when dealing with seldom heard groups (Lowe et al., 2023), who aren't traditionally captured by government research (but see Nicholson et al., 2022). As interactions between humans are increasingly moderated by machines, social scientists have begun to realise the importance of human or user-led design of digital media. For some this allows participatory research to be seen as part of a commitment to responsible innovation (Jirotka, 2017).[9]

Conclusion: How Might a User-Centred Transformation Project Look Different?

In this final section of the book, we look at alternative ways in which a user-centred digitalisation project might have been conceived in the hope that this will facilitate a different way of thinking in the future. In doing so, we recognise the many constraints that the Ministry of Justice are under and the challenging agenda they have had to implement when it was made clear that the digitalisation project could only be funded on the back of court closures. This has undoubtedly placed them in the extremely difficult position of having to introduce reforms which were unlikely to be reversed, without the time to determine their value and efficacy in terms of the experience of those using the legal system. In the midst of this demanding programme, there have been some notable successes including a number of online platforms which now support the public in navigating the requirements of getting a no-fault divorce or making a money claim. But rather than bowing to pragmatic concerns about the funding available, we return to a claim which will always be unpopular with the Treasury: that public services need to be funded at a level which allows them to deliver services to all citizens in ways that focus on public sector values around participation, accessibility, transparency, accountability, dignity and voice. The remainder of this section outlines four ways in which the reform programme currently drawing to a close, and those mounted in the future could be reconceived.

The first of these is taking the wealth of knowledge within the socio-legal community seriously. For many decades a significant proportion of socio-legal research has focused on the phenomenology of legal process from lay user perspectives. Literature in the field of legal consciousness, unmet legal needs, access to justice, procedural justice and lawyer–client relations have burgeoned as a result. This places scholars in the field in an excellent position to re-imagine what a user-centred approach to the transformation of the justice system might look like. The approach of HMCTS to evaluating the success of particular programmes has generally been to evaluate what is happening in partnership with private research agencies or to conduct research in-house. There are notable exceptions, but very little effort has been put into developing intra-public sector relationships with the socio-legal community. This includes the poor use made of the Ministry of Justice Court Reform Evaluation Committee set up for the purpose of bringing this expertise to bear. One impact of this is that it has stymied methodological innovation, with the emphasis being placed on post-implementation evaluations rather than participatory research project of the kind outlined above. This is despite the fact that this is an area where the academic sector is taking the lead in debate.

Secondly, insufficient attention has been paid to the lay user's journey through the justice system from beginning to end. This involves prioritising the needs of the public, or at the very least treating them as though their views were as important as the needs of professional users. Looking at the justice system from a public user perspective one might, for instance, question why the reform programme in England and Wales has focused on so many discrete jurisdiction-specific developments (see Table 1.1 in Chapter 1). It is undoubtedly the case that the English and Welsh justice system is highly fragmented with different policies, procedures and cultures across the different tribunal and court systems. There is often no particular logic underpinning the differences across the systems which have as much to do with legal history as anything else. This makes the introduction of unified systems and approaches complex, but for all its talk for revolutionary change, there appears to have been no attempt to rationalise the many different micro-legal systems in place which rarely if ever make sense to the lay user. One reason for this is that the idea of an integrated reform policy conflicts with the administrative and judicial boundaries of these microsites. The impact in Fishenden's (2023) words has been '...hard coding [of] silo policies, bureaucratic boundaries, funding, processes, and services of yesterday's world, presenting them in all their fragmented glory on to a screen' (p. iii).

The implications of this siloed approach are considerable. Research has suggested that people, especially those with complex lives, frequently approach the legal system with more than one legal problem. Unfair dismissal may for instance have led to re-possession and the need to appeal against a refused welfare benefit. Genn's (2019) research has found that there is growing evidence of bidirectional links between law and health suggesting that social and economic problems with a legal dimension can exacerbate or create ill health and that conversely ill health can create legal problems. As presently designed, and reinforced in the design of multiple digital platforms, this would require a citizen to use three different systems to assert their rights.

Thirdly, it is clear that a more transformative transformation would have involved greater attention being paid to the ways in which public or commercial goods and services at the heart of disputes could be improved as a result of the data being collected by the legal system. The implications of this go beyond the justice system to the government eco-system more generally, linking adverse events and identification of repeat problems in order to change service delivery for the general public good in the future. The introduction of siloed digital platforms and the historical lack of investment in collecting detailed data about the characteristics of litigated and prosecuted cases renders this an extremely challenging task. Despite this, there are examples of good practice which exist within the government sector. One of these is the Faculty of Learning, run by NHS Resolution which deals with all the claims made against the NHS. The purpose of this facility is to provide a repository of educational learning products and resources developed by NHS Resolution to support the health service to learn from the problems which litigation has drawn attention to. By way of example, the Faculty's module on consent draws attention to the fact that in a recent five-year period there were 1194 claims which hinged on inadequate consent being given at a cost to the NHS of £202 million. The site uses a series of videos and documents to support healthcare professionals in ensuring the consent process is managed more effectively. This example draws attention to the value of adopting an approach that achieves the effective resolution of a dispute for the individuals involved while also making sure that litigation can be used to serve the public good. Digitalisation and the production of large datasets make systemic change of this kind more possible than ever before.

Fourthly, we end the book where we started it, by thinking about the needs of disadvantaged users. There is a considerable body of socio-legal research which suggests that the disadvantaged have always had more problems identifying, initiating, and pursuing claims than those with more cultural, social and economic capital. HMCTS has acknowledged that some people find it difficult to access both offline and online services, but we question whether their existing support services adequately address the depth of need. By way of example, recent research in which qualitative interviews were undertaken with defendants in the criminal justice system, discovered a host of problems relating to accessibility and comprehensibility. These included a lack of relevant and user-friendly information provided by a trusted source; timely information to support more informed decision-making, particularly around legal representation; and inadequate information and signposting to services that could help defendants with their additional support needs such as mental health and housing issues. Recommendations arising from the research included the provision of concise information in EasyRead formats and somewhat ironically given that the research was commissioned by HMCTS, the re-introduction of queries desks at courts (Mullen et al., 2020).

A second larger scale study commissioned by HMCTS (2018) also found that the key user need across systems was increasing the visibility of the court and tribunal process and stages in the user journey. Having information on what to expect was an important factor in experiences across all jurisdictions and at all stages of the user journey. Research undertaken by Hanrahan (2021) into vulnerable user expectations of the criminal justice system also found that service users felt depersonalised, judged, and voiceless through their interactions with HMCTS. They also felt anxious, ashamed and afraid when engaging with courts and tribunals, struggled to understand information about courts and tribunals and processes and accessed help in navigating courts and tribunals processes (Hanrahan, 2021). These are not necessarily problems which can be easily resolved through telephone advice, especially where people have to rely on having enough phone credit to access call centres.

Without the injection of additional funding streams, it is unlikely that these problems will go away in the process of digitalisation. But one of the most worrying themes to emerge from this book is the many ways in which existing inequalities are being exacerbated by the shift to online services at the same time as austerity measures remain in place and the not-for-profit legal advice is struggling. Advice given in courts has been substituted with centralised call centre advice and some face-to-face advice is being delivered through a new Digital Support Service. However, research to date has shown that referrals to digital support services remain highly dependent on locally based face-to-face advice agencies (Good Things Foundation, 2020). The presence of a new national telephone helpline may make it easier for those who live in advice deserts to access help, but this change in the ways that support is organised assumes that telephone advice is as good as that which can be given locally by those who understand local cultures and context. This assumption has been cast into doubt in research by Burton (2018, 2020) which makes clear that both the general needs and the advice needs of the disadvantaged are complex, with advisers frequently needing to sift through such things as letters, demands and rent records before the full complexity of an issue can be understood. This is not easily managed on a phone line. The Good Things Foundation (2020, 2021) have argued that the additional emotional, procedural and legal support that centres provided during a pilot scheme was highly valued by users despite being outside the ambit of the current provision. Indeed, it was argued that in some instances not having this additional support would have been a barrier to accessing HMCTS services online. During the same pilot, 1274 public users were supported, the majority of whom were Social Security and Child Support (SSCS) appellants, which suggested that the economically disadvantaged were most likely to need help with online processes. Coupled with a lack of access to computers, adequate bandwidth, and phone credit, research in this vein demonstrates the many ways in which a two-tier system exists but is also set to be made worse if the needs of all users are not placed at the centre of future initiatives.

Notes

1. The UK government has recently launched a government secondment scheme with a view to attracting talented digital professionals into government to help transform their digital services https://www.civil-service-careers.gov.uk/ddat-digital-secondment-programme/.
2. A short demonstration of this can be found at (HMCTS, 2023a).
3. https://www.gov.uk/government/organisations/hm-courts-and-tribunals-service/about/research.
4. Three of these projects have been commissioned; two by Revolving Door and one by the Kantar group which has 25 global offices.
5. Responses to the survey came from judges (1140), legal representatives (2022) and HMCTS staff (358). In addition to members of the public interviews were conducted with judges (32), legal representatives (25) and HMCTS staff (25), intermediaries and support professions (11) and observers (9). See further Clark (2021).
6. For a definition of push to we survey see: https://www.ipsos.com/en/ipsos-encyclopedia-push-web-surveys.
7. Agile service design methods can be contrasted to traditional big bang 'waterfall' methods and focus on piecemeal development of digital services exposing designs t user feedback at an earlier stage of the process. See further the Government digital service standard; Web content accessibility guidelines 2.0; Digital Service Standard and the Technology code of practice.
8. The telephone service was being offered by HMCTS directly through the Courts and Tribunals Service Centres (CTSC).
9. In participatory design it is also important to feedback to participants the explanation for as to why some of their findings or requests have not been embedded into the final design, something that doesn't happen within current forms of consultation, as well as negotiating the at time competing demands of different participant groups (Mulcahy & Tsalapatanis, 2023).

Bibliography

Agile Software Development. (2001). *Principles Behind the Agile Manifesto.* http://agilemanifesto.org/principles.html

Allmann, K. (2022). *UK Digital Poverty Evidence Review.* Digital Poverty Alliance.

Bobbio, L. (2019). Designing Effective Public Participation. *Policy and Society, 38*(1), 41–57. https://doi.org/10.1080/14494035.2018.1511193

Breaugh, J., Hammerschmid, G., Rackwitz, M., & Singh, M. (2023). *What Does Private Sector Involvement in Government Digitalisation Mean for Public Values?* LSE Blog. https://blogs.lse.ac.uk/europpblog/2023/08/01/what-does-private-sector-involvement-in-government-digitalisation-mean-for-public-values/

Brewer, G. A., Neubauer, B. J., & Geiselhart, K. (2006). Designing and Implementing E-Government Systems: Critical Implications for Public Administration and Democracy. *Administration & Society, 38*(4), 472–499. https://doi.org/10.1177/0095399706290638

Burton, M. (2018). Justice on the Line? A Comparison of Telephone and Face-to-Face Advice in Social Welfare Legal Aid. *Journal of Social Welfare and Family Law, 40*(2), 195–215.

Burton, M. (2020). Lost in Space? The Role of Place in the Delivery of Social Welfare Law Advice over the Telephone and Face-to-Face. *Journal of Social Welfare and Family Law, 42*(3), 341–359.

Byrom, N., & Beardon, S. (2021). *Understanding the Impact of COVID-19 on Tribunals: The Experience of Tribunal Judges*. Legal Education Foundation. https://www.mentalhealthlaw.co.uk/media/2021-06-02_LEF_Understanding_the_the_impact_of_COVID-19_on_tribunals.pdf

Clark, J. (2021). *Evaluation of Remote Hearings During the COVID 19 Pandemic*. HM Courts and Tribunals Service. https://www.gov.uk/government/publications/hmctsremote-hearing-evaluation

Contini, F., & Lanzara, G. F. (2009). Introduction. In F. Contini & G. F. Lanzara (Eds.), *ICT and Innovation in the Public Sector: European Studies in the Making of E-Government* (pp. 1–6). Palgrave Macmillan UK. https://doi.org/10.1057/9780230227293_1

Deloitte. (2021). *Criminal Justice and the Technological Revolution*. https://www.deloitte.com/content/dam/assets-shared/legacy/docs/perspectives/2022/gx-deloitte-criminal-justice-and-technological-revolution-report.pdf

Fishenden, J. (2023). *Fracture: The Collision Between Technology and Democracy and How We Fix It*. Amazon.

Fletcher, A. (2023). And (Epistemic) Justice For All: A Cautionary Tale of Knowledge Inequality in Participatory Research. *Quality in Ageing and Older Adults* (ahead-of-print). https://doi.org/10.1108/QAOA-03-2023-0021

Fouzder, M. (2021, March 12). *HMCTS Apologises for CVP Connection Problem*. Law Society Gazette. https://www.lawgazette.co.uk/news/hmcts-apologises-for-cvp-connection-problems/5107762.article

Fricker, M. (2007). *Epistemic Injustice: Power and the Ethics of Knowing*. Oxford University Press. https://doi.org/10.1093/acprof:oso/9780198237907.001.0001

Genn, H. (2019). When Law Is Good for Your Health: Mitigating the Social Determinants of Health Through Access to Justice. *Current Legal Problems, 72*(1), 159–202.

Good Things Foundation. (2020). *HMCTS Digital Support Service: Implementation Review*. https://www.goodthingsfoundation.org/insights/hmcts-digital-support-service-implementation-review/

Good Things Foundation. (2021). *Digital Support: Phase 4 Addendum Report*. Good Things Foundation and HMCTS. https://www.goodthingsfoundation.org/wp-content/uploads/2021/08/GTF-HMCTS-Digital-Support-Phase-4-Addendum-Report-Aug-2021-v5-AW.pdf

Hagan, M. (2020). Legal Design as a Thing: A Theory of Change and a Set of Methods to Craft a Human-Centered Legal System. *Design Issues, 36*(3), 3–15. https://doi.org/10.1162/desi_a_00600

Hanrahan, A. (2021). *Identifying, Understanding, and Responding to the Multiple Complex Needs of Court Service Users*. HMCTS.

Hansen, A., & Koefoed Hansen, L. (2022). UI for When It Is No Longer U and I: An Online Divorce Form Rethought with Rites of Passage Theory. *Nordic Human-Computer Interaction Conference*, 1–12. https://doi.org/10.1145/3546155.3547280

HMCTS. (2018). *HM Courts & Tribunals Service Citizen User Experience Research*. Ministry of Justice. https://assets.publishing.service.gov.uk/media/5b28b78b40f0b634abe91325/HMCTS_Citizens_User_Experience_Research_June_2018.pdf

HMCTS. (2020). *Assessment Report Findings from the TV Licensing Pilot of the Behaviourally Redesigned Single Justice Procedure Notice*. https://assets.publishing.service.gov.uk/media/62e39f7ce90e07143b6ed790/SJPN_Redesign_Pilot_Report_-_TVL_FINAL_-_Accessible_version.pdf

HMCTS. (2021). *Evaluation of Remote Hearings During the COVID-19 Pandemic. Technical Appendix*. https://assets.publishing.service.gov.uk/government/uploads/system/uploads/attachment_data/file/1039520/Evaluation_of_remote_hearings_-_technical_appendix.pdf

HMCTS. (2022). *First-Tier Tribunal (Immigration and Asylum Chamber) Reform: Interim Process Evaluation*. https://assets.publishing.service.gov.uk/media/633c1668e90e074403e63180/First-tier_Tribunal__Immigration_and_Asylum_Chamber__Reform_interim_evaluation_final_report.pdf

HMCTS. (2023a). *Fact Sheet Video Hearing Service*. https://www.gov.uk/government/publications/hmcts-reform-infrastructure-and-enabling-services-fact-sheets/fact-sheet-video-hearings-service

HMCTS. (2023b). *Reducing the Heat: What to Expect from Our Online Divorce Service*. https://insidehmcts.blog.gov.uk/2023/11/17/reducing-the-heat-what-to-expect-from-our-online-divorce-service/

House of Commons Committee of Public Accounts. (2019). *Transforming Courts and Tribunals: Progress Review* (HC 27). https://publications.parliament.uk/pa/cm201919/cmselect/cmpubacc/27/27.pdf

House of Commons Justice Committee. (2019). *Court and Tribunal Reforms* (HC 190, Second Report of Session 2019). House of Commons. https://publications.parliament.uk/pa/cm201919/cmselect/cmjust/190/190.pdf

Jirotka, M., Grimpe, B., Stahl, B., Eden, G., & Hartswood, M. (2017). Responsible Research and Innovation in the Digital Age. *Communications of the ACM, 60*(5), 62–68. https://doi.org/10.1145/3064940

Lowe, K., Barajas, J., & Coren, C. (2023). "It's Annoying, Confusing, and It's Irritating": Lived Expertise for Epistemic Justice and Understanding Inequitable Accessibility. *Journal of Transport Geography, 106*, 103504. https://doi.org/10.1016/j.jtrangeo.2022.103504

Marti, P., & Bannon, L. J. (2009). Exploring User-Centred Design in Practice: Some Caveats. *Knowledge, Technology & Policy, 22*(1), 7–15. https://doi.org/10.1007/s12130-009-9062-3

Misra, S., Kumar, V., Kumar, U., Fantazy, K., & Akhter, M. (2012). Agile Software Development Practices: Evolution, Principles, and Criticisms. *International Journal of Quality & Reliability Management, 29*(9), 972–980. https://doi.org/10.1108/02656711211272863

Mulcahy, L., & Tsalapatanis, A. (2022). Exclusion in the Interests of Inclusion: Who Should Stay Offline in the Emerging World of Online Justice? *Journal of Social Welfare and Family Law, 44*(4), 455–476. https://doi.org/10.1080/09649069.2022.2136713

Mulcahy, L., & Tsalapatanis, A. (2023). Handmaidens, Partners or Go-Betweens: Reflections on the Push and Pull of the Judicial and Justice Policy Audience. *Oñati Socio-Legal Series*. https://doi.org/10.35295/osls.iisl.1707

Mullen, P., Collins, C., & Savage, K. (2020). *Understanding and Improving Defendant Engagement*. HMCTS. https://revolving-doors.org.uk/wp-content/uploads/2022/07/Understanding-and-improving-defendant-engagement.pdf

National Audit Office. (2018). *Early Progress in Transforming Courts and Tribunals* (HC 1001). https://www.nao.org.uk/wp-content/uploads/2018/05/Early-progess-in-transforming-courts-and-tribunals.pdf

National Audit Office. (2023). *Progress on the Courts and Tribunals Reform Programme* (HC 1130). https://www.nao.org.uk/wp-content/uploads/2023/02/progress-on-courts-and-tribunals-reform-programme-1.pdf

Nicholson, W., Juniper, J., Holloway, B., & Wingfield, K. (2022). *A Guide to Inclusive Social Research Practices* [Government Social Research Profession]. https://www.gov.uk/government/publications/a-guide-to-inclusive-social-research-practices/a-guide-to-inclusive-social-research-practices

Osei-Kyei, R., & Chan, A. (2015). Review of Studies on the Critical Success Factors for Public-Private Partnership (PPP) Projects from 1990 to 2013. *International Journal of Project Management, 33*(6), 1335–1346.

Rossner, M., & McCurdy, M. (2018). *Implementing Video Hearings (Party-to-State): A Process Evaluation*. Ministry of Justice.

Sanders, E. B.-N., & Stappers, P. J. (2008). Co-creation and the New Landscapes of Design. *CoDesign, 4*(1), 5–18. https://doi.org/10.1080/15710880701875068

Sheller, M. (2018). *Mobility Justice: The Politics of Movement in an Age of Extremes*. Verso Books.

Tsalapatanis, A., & Mulcahy, L. (2023). *Designing for Inclusion: How to Produce Inclusive Materials for Advice Sector Clients*. https://ora.ox.ac.uk/objects/uuid:6b1ddab7-0dca-45ff-be4a-eeffd6bf2a5b

Tsosie, R. (2017). *Indigenous Peoples, Anthropology, and the Legacy of Epistemic Injustice*. Routledge.

Vaughn, L. M., & Jacquez, F. (2020). Participatory Research Methods—Choice Points in the Research Process. *Journal of Participatory Research Methods, 1*(1). https://doi.org/10.35844/001c.13244

Index

A
Accessibility, 12
Access to justice, 39
Accountability, 79, 85
Advice deserts, 39
Agile design, 83–85
Alienation, 42
Architecture, 41, 43, 56, 58, 62, 64
Artificial intelligence, 2, 27, 28, 30, 40
As if technology, 23
Asynchronous hearings, 44

B
Bias, 29, 43
British and Irish Legal Information Institute, 23
Buildings, 41, 42, 46, 55–59

C
Citizen, 3, 11, 78–80, 85, 87
Citizens Advice, 24, 39
Civic, 1, 2, 15, 54–59, 61, 70
civil justice, 3–6, 8–10, 12, 13, 16–18
Civil money claims, 9
Cloud Video Platform, 61, 81
Co-design, 84
Common Platform, 8, 10
Consultation, 82, 84, 89
Court closure, 12, 42
Court reform, 10, 11, 13
Courtrooms, 41
Courts & Tribunals Service Centres, 10, 60
Courts and Tribunals Design Guide, 57, 59, 66
Criminal justice, 5, 9, 42, 43
Customer, 7, 11, 79
Cyberjustice lab, 40
Cyber-negotiation tools, 26
Cybersettle, 27

D
Defendant, 62, 65, 67, 69
Degradation rituals, 42
Digital case management systems, 41
Digital disadvantage, 13, 67
Digitally disadvantaged, 80, 83
Dignity, 57, 80, 85
Divorce, 8, 40, 54, 81
Dock, 42

E
eBay, 29
Efficiency, 5, 6, 9, 11, 24, 28, 38, 40, 41, 54, 55, 60, 70
Electronic filing, 24
Employment tribunals, 9
Epistemic injustice, 78, 83

INDEX

F
Family, 39
Family courts, 10, 54, 63
Filing, 5, 6

G
Good Things Foundation, 10, 88
Gravitas, 64

H
Holograph, 25
Hybrid hearings, 24, 54, 55, 62, 65

I
Immigration and asylum, 8

J
Journalism, 46
Journey, 84, 86
Judge, 55, 59, 62–64, 68, 70
JusticeBot, 28, 40

L
Lack of research, 14
lawyers, 28, 54, 60–62, 64, 66
Legal aid, 11, 54
Legal education, 23, 39
Leveson Report, 5
Litigants in person, 32, 83
Live streaming of trials, 45
Lord Chancellor's Department, 6
Lord Chief Justice, Baron Thomas of Cwmgiedd, 7
Lord Justice Auld, 5
Lord Justice Briggs, 12, 26
Lord Justice Burnett, 7, 12, 41

M
Money Claims Online, 24, 47, 54

N
Natural Language Processing, 28
Negotiations, 22, 26–28

New Public Management, 55, 78

O
Online dispute resolution, 38
Online forms, 40
Online hearings, 9, 24, 38, 43, 44, 46
Online platforms, 40
Open justice, 45, 56, 66, 67, 71

P
Pandemic, 11, 13, 14, 17, 45, 54, 63, 66, 68
Participation, 44, 79, 85
Participatory, 84–86, 89
Platform, 24, 26, 27
Platform capitalism, 2
Police, 4, 9
Police stations, 53, 62
Prisons, 62
Private sector, 11, 23, 27, 28, 78–81
Probate, 8, 24, 47, 54
Procedural justice, 63
Process pluralism, 45
Proportionality, 13
Public counters, 59

R
Rechtwijzer, 26
Resolver platform, 45
Ritual, 43, 55, 64, 70

S
screen, 8, 25, 61, 63, 69
Sightlines, 61
Silo, 86
Singapore, 6
Sir Geoffrey, Vos, 30
Situational disadvantage, 80
Social Security and Child Support, 8, 10, 24
Socio-legal, 14, 15, 86
Susskind, Richard, 6
Symbol, 56

T
Tax, 54

Threshold, 59
Traffic Penalty Tribunal, 44
Transforming Our Justice System
    Report, 7
Transparency, 46, 79, 82, 85

U
Underinvestment in the justice system, 3
User perspective, 84

V
video, 2, 5, 8, 11, 16, 62–65, 67, 68, 70

Videolink, 21, 24
Vulnerable users, 43

W
We Are Digital, 10
Webchat, 24, 32
Witness, 60, 61
Woolf, Lord, 4–6, 16
Woolf Reforms, 54

Y
Youstice, 40

GPSR Compliance

The European Union's (EU) General Product Safety Regulation (GPSR) is a set of rules that requires consumer products to be safe and our obligations to ensure this.

If you have any concerns about our products, you can contact us on ProductSafety@springernature.com

In case Publisher is established outside the EU, the EU authorized representative is:

Springer Nature Customer Service Center GmbH
Europaplatz 3
69115 Heidelberg, Germany

Batch number: 08133234

Printed by Printforce, the Netherlands